Ethical Dilemmas

Case Studies for Ethical Decision Making

Edited by

David Thorne

CONTENTS

Acknowledgments   6

Introduction   7

Prelude: Common Ethical Frameworks   11

One Bad Fight   19
By Jody A. Kunk-Czaplicki

International Secrets   49
By Xiaobin Dai

Church Planting Problems   65
By David Thorne

Office Dalliances   95
By Emmah M. Muema

The Good and the Bad Cop   121
By Oluwatobi Taiwo Ishola

The Caseworker's Dilemma   153
By Lakishia Huggins

Friends in High Places   169
By Andy Alt

About the Author   189

ACKNOWLEDGMENTS

Thank you to my amazing cohort for sharing your stories. I have looked forward to sharing every class with you. I will be forever changed by your insights, stories, and friendship.

Introduction

I feel honored to be a part of the Leadership Studies doctoral program at Bowling Green State University. Hearing perspectives on leadership, diversity, and ethics by individuals from Kenya, Nigeria, China, Bahrain, and Toledo, Ohio is a gift I wish all could receive.

In the spring of 2018, our doctoral cohort began a class on ethical leadership. The final project was to write a scenario containing an ethical dilemma. During our final class each student stood and shared complicated situations, often built upon deeply personal circumstances. I was amazed by each story and felt compelled to gather and share these scenarios for the benefit of all.

Reading the seven cases contained in this volume will be valuable for multiple reasons. First, each story gives perspective on the complicated decisions people make every day. Ethical dilemmas are everywhere. Reading through a scenario about a field you know very little about will increase your understanding of that field while increasing your compassion for the challenges individuals in that field face every day. Also, regardless of the field, we can learn a lot by observing how others navigate a morally murky situation. Their scenario might shed light on a similar situation we presently deal with, or could one day.

Second, reading ethical scenarios can help you uncover your own ethical value system. Ethical decisions are built on a system of codes or beliefs. As you work through each case you must face the question, "What would I do?" Your answers reveal glimpses into your personal values. Some will place a higher priority on relationships while others emphasize the completion of a task. Some are guided by principle while others prioritize situational factors. Those who do not understand their own personal values will have more trouble making decisions and could be more easily swayed to make decisions that go against what they hold most dear.

The third reason is to help develop your personal decision-making process. Understanding your personal value system is not sufficient. You must also figure out how to use your values to make ethical decisions. It is like learning how to drive. A person may know everything there is to know about a car from reading the manual, but that does not mean they know how to drive that car. Developing your personal decision-making process is like learning to drive your ethical car. As you read the scenarios within this book, you will witness how each author worked through the various viewpoints within their specific situation.

Reading through ethical situations reminds us not every decision is clear. Instead of living in a *right or wrong, black or white* world, we often find ourselves choosing between various shades of grey. As you read each case consider what you would do. Some cases share a resulting decision while others leave it up for reader interpretation. It is important to note that just because a scenario has concluding results does not mean the final decision made was the *correct* one. A reader will have to work through the facts of each case and make their own determination.

I hope you will enjoy reading each ethical scenario in this volume as much I did hearing them in my ethical leadership class. I hope each case will spark discussion and debate on what one should do in a similar situation. We need more discussion today on ethical decision-making. I believe this book is a helpful way to begin the conversation.

Prelude

Common Ethical Frameworks

Everyday people are forced to make decisions. Some are seemingly small, like whether to choose the peanut butter puff cereal or bran flakes for breakfast. But, other decisions come with consequences. Should you cheat on the test, reveal conflicting interests with your client, or honestly share your shortcomings with your boss? These complicated situations create competing values: the value of honesty with the value of self-preservation.

Author Mark Schwartz calls these *ethical issues* and writes, "An *ethical issue* is defined as a situation in which an individual must reflect upon competing moral standards and/or stakeholder claims in determining what is the morally appropriate decision or action" (2017, p, 10). This book contains seven scenarios comprised of multiple ethical issues.

Determining what to do in a morally murky situation can be challenging. The use of ethical frameworks can help navigate complicated moral dilemmas. An ethical framework is made up of various values useful in the ethical decision-making process. I'd like to briefly define the three most common ethical frameworks mentioned or used throughout the scenarios in this book. The definition of each framework will include a question common to the perspective and an example.

Teleological vs. Deontological

Summary: Choosing the greatest good or what is morally right, regardless of consequences.

Teleological: Believing the best choice is the one that produces the greatest good for the greatest number. Or, choices that produce the least harm (Callahan, 1988, p. 19).

Question: What will produce the greatest good for the most people in this situation?

Examples: *Telling your children or a partner that their new haircut looks good to boost their confidence, even though it does not. Or, an army general sending one soldier in to gather essential intelligence, even if that assignment will most likely result in their death.*

Deontological: Basing decisions on the moral or value of the choice, regardless of the consequences.

Question: What is the right (moral, legal, ethical) choice to make in this situation?

Examples: *Telling your children or partner that their haircut does not look good because it is the truth, regardless of the consequences. Or, when pulled over by a police officer, confessing that you were speeding and were doing so for no good reason.*

Ethic of Justice, Care and Critique

Summary: Making decisions based on an awareness of who benefits, what is just, and relationships with all people involved (Starratt, 1991).

Ethic of Critique: Investigating ethical dilemmas with an awareness of social inequalities. Decision-making with an awareness of power and structure complexities by asking, "Who benefits?"

Example: *Taking into consideration how gender and race influence the application of ethical hiring practices.*

Ethic of Justice: Asks, "How shall we govern ourselves?" Starratt notes this question could be applied to the individual or community (1991, p. 190). But he adds, "The ethic of justice demands that the claims of the institution serve both the common good and the rights of the individuals in the school" (1991, p. 194).

Example: *Ensuring there are effective policies in place to ensure ethical and equitable hiring practices.*

Ethic of Care: Reflecting on every decision's effect on relationships. Starratt writes, "This ethic places the human persons-in-relationship as occupying a position for each other of absolute value; neither one can be used as a means to an end" (1991, p. 195).

Example: *Considering the impact of hiring policies on potential employees and those making hiring decisions.*

Principle of Benefit Maximization vs. Principle of Equal Respect

Summary: Choosing the greatest good or decisions focused on what's best for each individual.

Principle of Benefit Maximization: Similar to the deontological framework, this principle focuses on decisions that result in the most good or "the greatest benefit for the most people" (Strike, Haller, & Soltis, 2005, p. 17).

Question: What will produce the greatest good for the most people in this situation?

Example: *A city might enact a law disallowing cars to park on the street overnight for various reasons even though a few houses in the city only have a small driveway.*

Principle of Equal Respect: Considers the intrinsic value of every person. Strike et al. writes that this principle, "requires that we act in ways that respect the equal worth of moral agents" (2005, p. 17). They propose that this principle can be summed up through the Golden Rule: treating others in the same way we wish to be treated.

Question: How would I like to be treated in a similar situation?

Example: *A school administrator considering the story and circumstance of an individual who is in the office for punching a fellow student before dispensing punishment.*

Reading Ethical Scenarios

As you read through the following ethical scenarios, keep these frameworks in mind. Also, consider what ethical values drive the decisions of each character. In the end, consider what you believe should be done, or what you would have done in a similar circumstance and why.

This list of ethical frameworks is by no means exhaustive. But, it can serve as a reference for the most commonly mentioned frameworks used throughout the following scenarios.

References

Callahan, J. C. (1988). *Ethical issues in professional life*. New York: Oxford University Press.

Schwartz, M. S., & Ohio Library and Information Network. (2017). *Business ethics: An ethical decision-making approach* (1st ed.). Malden, MA: Wiley Blackwell.

Starratt, R. J. (1991). Building an ethical school: A theory for practice in educational leadership. *Educational Administration Quarterly, 27*(2), 185-202.

Strike, K. A., Haller, E. J., & Soltis, J. F. (2005). *The ethics of school administration* (3rd ed.). New York: Teachers College Press

Chapter 1

One Bad Fight

by Jody A. Kunk-Czaplicki
Ithaca, New York

Definitions:
Temporary Suspension: An interim measure imposed by a student conduct administrator before any investigation or fact- finding process. This interim measure is used rarely. The student cannot attend classes, be on university property, nor participate in any university sponsored events.

Student Conduct Administrator: A professional who imposes interim measures, investigates, and adjudicates alleged acts of misconduct.

Accused Student: The student who allegedly participate in the behaviors alleged

Complainant: The person who was the victim of the alleged conduct of the accused.

Witnesses: Persons who have direct observations of the alleged incident

FERPA: Family Education Right to Privacy Act. This act requires confidentiality of all educational records for students who are enrolled in post-secondary institutions. Disciplinary files/records are educational records.

Characters:
Anne: The student conduct administrator

Jamie: The accused student

Mr. Frank: Jamie's attorney

Sam: The Complainant

Privae University: The private university

One Bad Fight

Student conduct administrators must demonstrate readiness, clear-headedness, judiciousness, and a steely resolve for all types of issues that come before them: acts of violence, entrenched parents, curious media inquiries, argumentative attorneys, and well-intentioned but misguided colleagues. The following is a matter that came to Anne's attention during her tenure as a student conduct officer at Privae University. Privae University is a small private college, situated in New City, Ohio. The questions it raised allowed reflection into professional and leadership values.

The Assault

Privae University's police officers called Anne to report that a one of the institutions' students, Jamie, had just been arrested for physical assault. Anne learned the following from this phone call: At approximately 2:00 a.m. earlier that same day outside a city bar, Jamie with a closed fist allegedly punched Sam on the side of the head, which resulted in Sam falling to the ground. Jamie then proceeded to kick Sam's body with his foot until a third party intervened.

When the city police department responded to the bar, Sam was not responsive. Jamie was currently being processed by the city police department. Jamie would be arraigned the next business day where bail would likely be set; however, Jamie would spend the night in jail. Jamie is a 21-year-old senior and a well-known Privae University student-athlete.

Sam had been transported to the local and regional hospital and was in critical but stable condition. Sam is 20-year-old, junior, student-athlete at a neighboring college. Sam's parents lived approximately 2 hours away and were on their way to be with Sam at hospital. Preliminary reports show Sam suffered a broken nose, fractured jaw, concussion, and potential kidney damage, though the results were inconclusive at that time. Sam had given oral statements to the police but had not signed any written statements.

Witnesses

Jamie desired an attorney and, therefore, had not made any remarks to the police upon Jamie's arrest. Privae Police Department had worked with the New City police to receive written statements by those in the bar that evening. The student conduct officer reviewed written statements from a myriad of witnesses (some of Jaime and Sam's friends, some with no relationship to either party). The student conduct officer learned the following:

(a.) Jamie and Sam were known to each other as their teams played against one another, though they were in different athletic divisions.

(b.) Before midnight, Jamie and Sam exchanged heated words while inside the bar.

(c.) A third-party, Jo (friend of Jamie), reported that Sam used a racial epithet toward Jaime which angered Jaime. Jo observed Jaime become hostile and agitated toward Sam.

(d.) Upon hearing these words, Jamie walked toward Sam and demanded that Sam leave the bar. Sam did not move and orally told Jamie that he refused to leave as he had done nothing wrong (an aside: the specific language Sam used was much more colorful and involved curse-words).

(e.) Jo reported the specific words Sam used. And as a result, Jo chose to stand between Sam and Jamie until each person walked away.

(f.) Two by-standers reported that as Sam walked away he yelled at Jamie, cursed at Jamie and remarked to Jamie that "You better watch your back because I know people."

(g.) Jo and Jamie observed that Sam continued to drink throughout the night. Jo reported that

Jamie had two more beers. Jo reported that Jamie did not seem intoxicated.

(h.) Jo left the bar a few minutes before Jamie and as they planned to get pizza on the walk home.

(i.) Mack, Sam's friend, was standing outside the bar as Jamie left the bar. Sam followed Jamie out. Mack reports that he saw Jamie "trip" but Jamie did not fall to the ground. As Jamie stood back up, Sam was moving away from Jamie. Jamie moved toward Sam. Mack reports he saw Jamie punch Sam with his closed fist on the side of Sam's head which resulted in Sam falling to the ground. Jamie proceeded to kick Sam with his foot until a third party removed Jamie.

(j.) The third party has not yet given a written statement, though police are in process.

Phone Calls

With that evidence, Anne analyzed if she would temporarily suspend Jamie from Privae University. To impose this interim measure, Anne needed to analyze two prongs as articulated by

Privae's Campus Code of Conduct (1.) was this an extraordinary circumstance? and (2.) was this the only measure necessary to ensure public order and safety.

Certainly, allegations of physical assault which resulted in a significant injury met the standard of extraordinary circumstances. This behavior, given its severity, could not be tolerated in Privae's community. It was the second prong that caused Anne pause. Anne chose to sleep on the decision and speak with her colleagues the next morning.

Upon Anne's arrival to her office, Anne received a phone call Mr. Frank, Jamie's attorney. Anne had worked with Mr. Frank before and experienced him to be an ethical and respectable local attorney, though a zealous advocate for his clients. Anne also had phone messages from Sam's parents, and Privae University's Police Department (Privae PD).

Anne responded to Privae PD first. The police reported that Anne would likely be receiving a copy of a signed statement from Jamie, Sam, and the third-party witness by the close of business and that Jamie's arraignment in the city court would be at 1:00 p.m. that afternoon.

Anne called Mr. Frank's requesting a full FERPA release before she spoke with him about details, mentioning acts of violence are taken very seriously by her office. Next, Anne returned Sam's parents call. They were appropriately distressed for the health of their son, worried about his future academic goals, and wanted immediate action from Privae University.

Considerations

Anne analyzed the following questions. These are ethical considerations. Most immediately, Anne analyzed the standard of temporary suspension. In considering this analysis, Anne asked herself the following questions:

> (1.) What weight, if any, should be given to the fact that the injured party is <u>not</u> a Privae University student?

> (2.) What weight, if any, should be given to the alleged act of provocation?

> (3.) Is there any other interim measure that Anne could impose, before due process,

that would preserve the public order and safety, protect the rights of the accused, and safety of the complainant?

(4.) Mr. Frank will raise that a University can never <u>ensure</u> public order and safety. Therefore, he will argue, that the standard of the temporary suspension has not been met. Knowing that, indeed, Mr. Frank is correct (i.e., a universities role is to <u>preserve</u> public order and safety, not to ensure it) how does Anne make the argument while meeting the expressed standard in Privae's Code?

(5.) Also, as a secondary strategy, Mr. Frank will encourage his client to take a medical leave from Privae for the semester, thereby preserving his academic record. Can Anne accept a medical leave in lieu of a temporary suspension?

Ethical Concerns and the Code

In examining each of the elements articulated in the Code: (1.) was this an extraordinary circumstance? and (2.) was this the only measure necessary to ensure public order and safety? Before examining each element, a critique or deconstruction is first warranted. Once deconstructed, Anne could align the information in such a way that balanced the right of the accused person, Jamie, the complainant Same, and the Privae University community.

Perhaps, this deconstruction and reconstruction would broaden or narrow how Privae's Code had been operationalized before, perhaps it would not. However, before Anne made a decision, she wanted to have clear reasoning, not only to serve an end in this case but also for the greater benefit of the community whom she served.

As Anne began her analysis, she realized that before she began to examine the two-pronged approach of 'extraordinary' and 'public order and safety', she needed to reconcile what weight she would place, if any, on a non-University complainant.

On one hand, allegedly assaulting a community member raised her concern of extraordinary. Not exemplifying the high standards of our community toward others outside our community indicated disturbing lack of judgement, and a lack of care toward the broader public. On the other hand, Anne knew of cases where the Privae community, via another conduct body, held a non-university complainant as less entitled to protection than a university community complainant.

Ethically, Anne found the university hearing board's reasoning problematic, as the analysis explored factors outside the alleged conduct of the accused person. This past case was considered precedent, however, Anne noted the alleged violence in the past case was not as severe as this violence alleged in the current case.

Anne analyzed this philosophical underpinning as an ethical decision from an ethic care: care as articulated toward the broader community. Though Anne understands how other reasonable minds could reasonably disagree, it was an important office policy decision to evaluate humanity higher than a specific status.

Community Equality

Anne concluded that the status of the complainant, as city community member, would not hold weight in her decision. Anne would not weigh the complainant's lack of Privae community membership in favor of imposing a 'lighter' interim measure on Jamie. Sam's relationship to the Privae community would not mitigate Jaime's behavior. Anne would focus on Jamie's alleged conduct. If Anne weighed the complainant's status as a mitigating factor here, Anne may open the door to an analysis that a deceased complainant had no standing due to his/her/their status as deceased.

Though certainly a strategy to bely credulity, Anne knew it would be used by a future zealous defense attorney. As such, Anne did not want her analysis to undermine future direction of the office.

Anne understood her decision may broaden Privae University's interpretation of a 'complainant'. However, in review of the Code, nothing prohibited her interpretation; the Code was silent. Since, for the time being, the buck stopped with Anne, she felt comfortable moving the Privae community in this direction. After using the ethic of care to establish the complainant's standing, Anne felt more comfortable examining the two-pronged approach through reviewing similar cases of alleged conduct and then speaking with trusted colleagues about their analysis.

An Extraordinary Circumstance

First, Anne examined if this matter was an extraordinary circumstance. In examining the definition of extraordinary circumstance, she began by examining the culture and climate of Privae. This environmental scan provided her valuable information on how the community had interpreted extraordinary in the past.

Anne's examination included reviewing past precedent and speaking with campus colleagues. When she reviewed past precedent, Anne found cases which had similar facts: a fight in the city (not on-campus), significant injury which required hospitalization, involving a student athlete, a claim of provocation but eventually unsubstantiated. Anne felt comfortable knowing she had reasonable precedent supporting a decision to temporarily suspension Jamie, however, the case in precedent involved a complainant who was a Privae University student. This case involved a complainant who was not a Privae community member.

Since she felt comfortable with her initial decision of evaluating human dignity over a person's role and status within a particular community, she could justify use of this case as precedent. Knowing that her potential decision may reinterpret or broaden the operational definition of 'extraordinary' based on the non-University complainant, Anne spoke with a few trusted colleagues about this and their subsequent analysis of aggravating and mitigating circumstances.

Colleague Insight

Anne spoke with three colleagues: the former director of student conduct, Joan; Privae

University's Chief of Police, Elizabeth; and the Vice President for Student Affairs, Brian. Though the decision was solely Anne's to make, she wanted to employ the concept of critique to analyze the decision from a different perspective.

She chose Joan, Elizabeth, and Brian as they collectively knew the Privae community well, had experience analyzing and evaluating competing priorities, and frankly, Anne wanted some degree of collegial support given the potential for broad scrutiny.

Former Director of Student Conduct, Joan

First, Anne spoke with Joan. Joan had been the prior director for 17 years and had experience analyzing how to reinterpret, broaden, or narrow operational definitions of the Code. Joan employed the concept of being ethical by doing ethical things. Others in Joan's position may have immediately accepted, or volunteered that Jamie take a medical leave, in lieu of a temporary suspension.

This would 'solve' a host of problems: the accused person would not be on campus, the director could say to the Sam and his parents that the accused student is not currently taken classes at Privae and is not in the city, and a no-contact order would be the least restrictive interim measure imposed on Jamie prior to a fair process.

This certainly was an option as Joan examined the matter. However, something stuck with Joan, as it did with Anne, does this approach have integrity to the Code, integrity to our community of scholars, or was it just the outcome that maximized the benefit the two individuals involved? Joan's professional definition of ethical behavior, though different than her operational, daily definition, employed a thoughtful analysis of weighing competing priorities. Joan focused on the objective information, known to date.

For Joan, the alleged conduct was extraordinary on its face. Joan explained that if the conduct were not as violent, perhaps she would have evaluated the complainant's status differently. Said a slightly different way, Joan interpreted extraordinary in a plain reading, and if the alleged violence had borderline evidence, the status of the complainant may provide some weight.

Though Anne understood Joan's analysis of extraordinary and Anne appreciated her focus on the alleged behavior of the accused student, she did not fully agree with the weighted perspective of the complainant's role. Anne viewed the complainant's status independently from the alleged conduct, not as a confounding variable.

Next, Anne spoke with Elizabeth, Privae University's Chief of Police. Elizabeth held this position for the past 10 years, however, had worked in the Privae community for almost 20 years. Elizabeth analyzed the matter from a criminal justice perspective, as her role suggested.

Chief of Police, Elizabeth

Elizabeth, like Joan, knew the Privae community well. Elizabeth evaluated the political and environmental context very high. She placed considerable weight on the following: Privae's strong value of employing a fair process; the trepidation of the community, via the hearing board, to uphold a temporary suspension for a matter that occurred off-campus; the potential for increased media involvement due to the role of student athletes; and the optics of a privileged complainant and a less privileged accused student. Anne appreciated Elizabeth's analysis of the political implications; this is a stark reality.

Elizabeth, in her role as Chief of Police of Privae University, had not only a duty to the broader community's justice system, but also to Privae's special community of scholars. Elizabeth viewed the facts of the matter as strong, however, the weight of the values, mores, and climate of Privae weighed heavily.

Ultimately, she concluded that the complainant's status as a non-Privae community member was irrelevant, however, the location of the alleged incident and the alleged acts of provocation weighed heavily. Said a different way, Elizabeth believed the conduct was not quite extraordinary given the degree of provocation and the Privae community's safety could be maintained through a persona non grata, a robust no-contact order, and a minimum one year leave of absence.

Elizabeth reiterated that the alleged conduct, if proven, was dangerous, troubling, and beyond any good judgement of a Privae student. Anne asked Elizabeth if the alleged conduct, on its face, without consideration of allegation of provocation rose to the level of a persona non grata.

Elizabeth affirmed that the level of violence was troubling and particularly chilling. Elizabeth's blended perspective of balancing the rights, responsibilities, and incorporating mitigating and aggravating circumstances employee a strong ethic of justice. The balance, for Elizabeth, hung on how the ethic of justice is manifested in a broader political environment.

Anne appreciated Elizabeth's perspective of aggravating and mitigating circumstances. This approach made good sense. However, Anne needed to divorce herself from the analysis of the potential political fallout. That analysis, and the response to it, would come once Anne's decision was made. Elizabeth was right, though, to remind Anne that a fair process was the pinnacle value of the Privae community. However, in Elizabeth's own words, the alleged conduct alone rose to the level of a persona non grata.

This piece of Elizabeth's analysis carried great weight to Anne. Anne wanted to better understand how others evaluated this weight. As such, she decided to speak with Privae's Vice President for Student Affairs, Brian. Generally, Anne wanted to know how much weight Brian allocated to mitigating circumstances and how his analysis impacted this specific case. Before Anne spoke with VPSA Brian, she decided to re-evaluate what facts she had, what facts she needed, and what ethical principles her analysis would heavily evaluate.

Interpreting the Facts

Upon review of the information, Anne knew the following: Jamie and Sam knew each other (i.e., this was not a random act of violence); Jamie has no disciplinary history at Privae (i.e., no need for escalation due to prior findings of violation); Sam has spent two days in the hospital with significant, life altering injuries; Mack, though friends with Sam, reported Jamie struck Sam about the head multiple times once Sam was already lying on the ground; Jo, though friends with Jamie, reports hearing Sam call Jamie a racial slur and generally threaten Jamie. Jamie was still incarcerated as he did not have the financial resources to make bail.

With this information, Anne compared and contrasted Joan and Elizabeth's analysis of extraordinary circumstances with her own. Joan and eventually Elizabeth conceded that the conduct itself was extraordinary. Joan believed the conduct on its face met the standard, regardless of the mitigating circumstances.

Elizabeth had a slightly different interpretation, the mitigating circumstance matter, the question for Elizabeth was how much weight to give to these circumstances. Anne's analysis fell between the two. On one hand, Anne wanted to isolate Jamie's behavior to apply an ethic of justice; excessive force resulting in significant injury meant a temporary suspension. However, given her application of an ethic of care to 'benefit' Sam, Anne felt compelled to apply a similar analysis toward Jamie.

Anne could understand how Jamie felt legitimately humiliated, threatened, and scared.

Anne could accept this defense for some degree of physicality. What was most troubling to Anne, however, was the number of chances Jamie had to stop his behavior. Anne was not satisfied with mitigating all of Jamie's behavior due to provocation, however, Anne was comfortable with mitigating some. The question then became how much and to what end?

Vice President Brian

Anne approached Vice President Brian with this question. Brian was relatively new to Privae, however, had been a Vice President of Student Affairs at public institution. As a part of his portfolio at this public institution, Brian oversaw student conduct as an appeal body.

Brian has spent a good portion of his professional life working directly with student conduct. The key difference, perhaps philosophically, is the difference between working at a public institution and a private institution. Though Privae functions as a private institution, the influence of the law school on the due/fair process of the conduct process, via the policy body, is an important value and strong indication of Privae's culture. Brian, though not on the job long, had a strong understanding of the broad competing priorities of this matter and the broader precedent determinations.

As Anne provided Brian with the details of the matter and her decisions thus far, Anne asked him how he evaluated mitigating and aggravating circumstances. Vice President Brian began by acknowledging he was not looking for equity between aggravating and mitigating (i.e., it is not a zero-sum analysis). Anne appreciated the reminder that the mitigating need not equal out the aggravating, or that the nature of the mitigating circumstances would mean a temporary suspension is not appropriate.

First, Brian began looking at the broader picture. Violence was not a community value; violence is intolerable. For Brian, the greatest threat to the safety of Privae's community is knowing, deliberate, thoughtful violence. To Brian, the greatest weight was the mindset, as evaluated by the behaviors, of the accused person. In viewing the information in the most favorable light to Jamie, the accused, he felt humiliated, harassed, threatened, and frightened. Certainly, this is a human reaction.

Again, for the sake of argument, Anne (like Brian) could understand if Jamie pushed Sam to the ground after these threats as Jamie left the bar to get himself to a safer location. However, what Brian and Anne both viewed as aggravating circumstances, were the alleged repeated strikes to the Sam's body after Sam was no longer a physical threat to Jamie. Brian believed this case warranted a temporary suspension.

The two remaining issues for Anne's consideration were (1.) If Anne would accept a health leave in lieu of a temporary suspension, and (2.) Would Mr. Frank's technical argument that a university can never ensure public order and safety hold merit? Anne evaluated Mr. Frank's last argument as the weakest amongst his arguments, and Anne knew this was a strategy often employed by Mr. Frank.

If Anne issued a temporary suspension, Mr. Frank (on behalf of Jamie) would likely appeal and he and Anne would argue the standard of a "duty of care" and how to interpret "ensure." Fundamentally, Anne's argument articulated an implied duty of care in ensure, via maintain.

Mr. Frank would argue that universities cannot ever ensure safety after an alleged act of violence, and as such, temporary suspensions should only be used in cases of campus wide violence where violence is imminent (not as a reaction to "highly disputed behavior.")

Anne always enjoyed this argument raised by Mr. Frank as he was advocating throwing out fair (or due) process (i.e., temporarily suspending a student before the behavior occurred). Outside of the presence of the student of whom he was representing, he would also smile wryly at Anne's response.

She recognized that Mr. Frank's job was to harness the evidence in a way most favorable to his client. Anne's duty, however, was to the integrity of Code, the process, the community, and her professional credibility. Anne's response demonstrated her professional ethical code which must stay aligned in interpreting, weighing, and evaluating the information (not harnessing the facts toward a specific end).

Final Decisions

For Anne, the remaining decision was the toughest. Would Anne accept a health leave in lieu of a temporary suspension? Anne truly could see the argument from both ways. On one hand, accepting a health leave, instead of a temporary suspension, met the goals of the complainant and the community: Jamie would not be at Privae, there would be a transcript notation that a judicial matter was pending on Jamie's transcript.

In past circumstances, the health leave process, organized out of Privae's health center, was liberally applied when students decided to take time away from their studies due to their concern about their health.

At a minimum, the student could not return for two consecutive semesters. In Anne's tenure at Privae, this was the first time a health leave would be taken after a student was incarcerated. Accepting a health leave, in lieu of a temporary suspension, would also meet Jamie's goals: it would maintain his academic record, offer a compassionate, humanistic response (and would engender a relationship toward, perhaps, a swift amicable resolution for the underlying matter).

On the other hand, accepting a health leave in lieu of issuing a temporary suspension would set precedent. Also, on principle, this would not be a common practice. A temporary suspension meant something different than a health leave. Anne wondered if she could find a creative solution that fit the needs of this case yet did not establish precedent. As Anne reflected on this, she kept thinking about how badly she wanted to punt this decision by not imposing the temporary suspension.

Embedded in this thought was her answer: Anne would rather not impose a temporary suspension than accept a health leave in lieu of one. Anne's thoughts and feelings had exposed her decision: Anne chose to impose a temporary suspension. For Anne, these two avenues of separation were different: the health leave implied the student took time off for a health-related problem, a temporarily suspension was a University response to an alleged act of serious violence). Anne would not accept a health leave in lieu of a temporary suspension.

Though Anne never took these decisions lightly, Anne felt at peace with her decision: to impose a temporary suspension on Jaime. Anne felt comfortable with this decision, yet she acknowledges that at a different time, and in a different place, she may have evaluated the facts differently, accepted a health leave instead of a temporary suspension. For Anne, at that time and in that place, the integrity to the Code, broadening the interpretation of the Code in one way, but not in another served as a principled, effective, and balanced ethical leader that her community needed.

Ethical Dilemmas

Chapter 2

International Secrets

by Xiaobin Dai
China

Definitions:
Center for International Education: Organization of State University dedicated to helping international students with their educational goals

Student Conduct Administrator: A professional who imposes interim measures, investigates, and adjudicates alleged acts of misconduct.

State University: Public university where the dilemma takes place.

Complainant: The person who was the victim of the alleged conduct of the accused.

Characters:
Lin: A graduate assistant from China who works for CIE

Lulu: An international student from China

Mr. Brown: Dean of International Education

Ming: An international student from China (Lulu's boyfriend)

International Secrets

In the summer of 2007, I received an offer to attend State University. As a Chinese citizen, I was nervous to travel to America for the first time. I set out on my journey with 3 large suitcases and a passion for learning. On the plane I gazed out the window thinking about my parent's sacrifice. I knew they were spending most of their savings to send me to school overseas. I felt the weight of this responsibility and was determined to meet their expectations.

I began classes that fall and worked as a graduate assistant in the Center for International Education (CIE). State University had only recently begun recruiting International students, so many of their processes seemed clunky and primitive. There were only three full-time employees in the office. As a graduate assistant, my job duty was basically assisting people whenever and wherever was needed.

Translating admission documents from Chinese to English was one of my tasks, I was a translator before I came to State University, so my supervisor had never doubted my translation. I enjoyed translating those documents until one day I had to translate something troubling.

Translating Secrets

It was an afternoon, Mr. Brown handed me an envelope and told me to translate the files. The envelope was mailed from China to Lulu, with some of her hospital records, a doctor note, and a letter from her parents. According to her doctor note, she had to do an appendix surgery and it took 2-4 weeks to recover; her parent's letter requested the school to give her excused sick leave, so she could go back to China for the surgery. Being from China, I started worrying about her when I saw these documents. I even thought about checking in on her.

Soon after, I saw Lulu in the cafeteria at dinner time and asked if she was all right, explaining how I was translating her documents. Lulu was upset and walked me to a corner where nobody was around. She told me she was about to do a surgery, but it was not appendix; it was an abortion. Her parents did not know, nor did the parents of her boyfriend Ming.

All the documents, including a forged doctor note, were made by their friends in China. She begged me not to let CIE know. She shared how she trusted me and she needed help. She said both her and Ming's parents had spent a lot of money for them to study in America. If they knew she was pregnant they would force them both to return to China and might cut their financial support. Both sets of parents would be severely disappointed in them.

On top of this, their parents would be talked about by their parents' friends and relatives. This would lead to great social embarrassment, making it very difficult to continue living in that environment. She began to cry. I was moved by her story because I knew everything she said was true. But what should I do?

Morally speaking, I should keep quiet because Lulu was in a hard situation. In addition, it was not my job to tell determine the veracity of each document. However, not telling the truth is against my code of ethics and school rules. I was in this dilemma. I decided to translate the documents without telling anything to anybody. I do not know if I made the right choice.

Analysis

The following analysis is written in the format of classroom discussion, which includes three constructs-justice, care, and honesty. Students will be divided into four groups to analyze this case, they will offer the ethical pros and cons of the choice Lin made, and some other possibilities that might happen at that time. This is a fictional scenario; all names are not real.

Ethic of Justice

Teacher: We have read the case, a big dilemma! We'll start with theories, then move on to discussion. Can anybody think of any justice theories that we can use to analyze the dilemma?

Group A: I'm thinking teleological and deontological theories.

Teacher: Very good. Let's review these theories. Anybody want to read the quote from the book please?

Group A: Teleological theory is the view that "we should always choose that which will tend to produce the greatest good for the greatest number" (Callahan, 1988, p.19). Teleological theories are consequentialist theories, which are "theories which hold that the moral value of an action or practice is a function of the consequences (real or probable) of that action or practice" (Callanhan, 1988, p.19). The deontologist denies what the teleologist asserts (Callahan, 1988).

Teacher: Now let's move on to discussion. What do you think Lin should do, and why?

Group A: On teleological grounds, I would argue that Lin should tell the truth to CIE. What if something happens, for example, complications after abortion surgery or air accident, State University will have to be responsible for not screening the fraud documents and approving the leave. If Lin tells the truth, CIE may contact their parents and choose a better and safer way to handle it.

Group B: I agree that Lin should tell the truth to CIE because if an employee finds fraud documents, CIE has the right to be informed.

Group C: I would suggest her not to tell the truth. What if Lin tells the truth, Lulu and Ming might be expelled because of submitting fake documents. Do not forget, they are from a country that has a very conservative history. Both them, their families might be criticized. If they go back without getting the degree, it will not be easy for them to find a job and support themselves. What if they are depressed, and maybe commit suicide. This result is not good for anybody.

Group D: I think Lin just needs to do her assigned job-translating. It is not her job to screen the documents. If Lin's supervisor tells her to screen the documents, then she should tell, if not, she does not have to.

Group B: But what if CIE finds out eventually? Lin will have consequences from State University if she does not tell the truth. Even though it is not Lin's duty to screen the documents, she has the knowledge of sick leave fraud and forgery, she should tell. It is not fair to Lin if she gets expelled or loses her job because of not telling.

Ethic of Care

Teacher: Very good discussion. I'm so glad you debated each choice on the grounds of teleological and deontological theories. Can we think about it in a view of care? How do you apply ethic of care theories to defend your choice?

Group A: I would say Lin should help Lulu because they are good friends and Lulu trusts her. Galligan writes that "when interdependence exists between people, they are motivated to act responsively toward self and others and thus to sustain connectivity...and an ethic of care" (Galligan, 1982, p. 149). If Lin wants to keep the relationship with Lulu, she should keep the secret.

Group B: Also, in Beck's reading, he mentions that caring always involves a willingness to accept another's reality uncritically (Beck, 1994). If Lin cares about her friend Lulu, then she is not supposed to judge what is good or bad for Lulu, all she needs to do is translating. Just like what Buber (1965) says, when you receive the other, you are totally with the other.

Group C: It is a little hard for me to say which choice shows care. According to Mayeroff (1971), to care for someone, you must know how to respond to what the person's needs and what our own powers and limitations are. I would like to defend the truth telling because Lin should know that Lulu needs her family to stand with her, what if something happens during surgery that needs her parents to make decisions for her. Abortion surgery can be dangerous, Lulu needs family support. On the other hand, I can use Mayeroff to argue against truth telling. Lin has the power to keep the secret for Lulu, and that's all Lulu needs. Lulu probably thinks that if Lin cares about her, she should just let her go. See, I can apply Mayeroff's theory to both sides, I am not sure which is the better choice.

Group A: Let's see what Harper Lee (1960) says about care, "you never really understand a person until you consider things from his point of view" (p. 34). It becomes easier, Lin should help Lulu if she cares about Lulu.

Group D: I think the choice will lean towards not telling the truth if we consider the topic of care. If Lin cares about Lulu, she should make sure Lulu feels she is not alone because she is understood, and someone is with her.

Honesty

Teacher: Great discussion, if time permits I will let you keep going, I really enjoy your argument, but now we have to move on to our next topic. Please think about honesty and noble lie, how do you defend or argue your choice?

Group A: I still do not think Lin should tell, because Carr (1968) suggests that there is no obligation to stop and consider who is going to get hurt. If the law says he can do it, that's all the justification he needs. There's nothing unethical about that. Since not telling the fraud is not violating the law, Lin does not have to tell CIE about it.

Group B: According to Ellin (1982), I think not telling the truth or withholding the truth, no less than lying, harms a person's interest in having true beliefs, in having the information necessary to make intelligent decisions, in not being manipulated, and in being regarded with respect. If CIE is not told the truth, they would not make the correct decision that they should have made. State University may be sued because of the incorrect decision if accidents happen to Lulu. I would say Lin should not lie to her employer.

Group C: But Bok (1978) says lying is excusable when undertaken for "noble" ends. Lin does not tell the truth because she does not want Lulu to be expelled or be criticized by her family, she wants Lulu to complete her degree and lives a better life. This is a "noble" end, so even Lin does not tell the truth, she is excusable.

Group D: I think Lin should be honest if that is her personal code of ethics. If Lin knows the documents are fake and does not tell, then she is not honest. She needs to be honest to her employer and to herself. Other than telling or not telling, I think Lin has another choice. Since the documents have been translated, she could tell Lulu to take them back. She should suggest Lulu to get support from her family, her family does not want Lulu to lose the opportunity of education and it is possible for them to request a family excuse from school. I think this may be the best result.

Teacher: Thank you students for your discussion. Everybody has theoretical support for their views. Our goal is not to decide which choice is better, we just need to think about as many possible solutions as possible. You all did a great job! Now the last question, if you were Lin, would you tell or not?

Class Results: Overall, 20% of students voted they would tell while 80% of students said they would not tell.

Summary

This case analysis is in a format of class discussion. In the class, students talk about ethics of justice (teleological versus deontological theories), ethic of care (theories of Galligan/Beck/Mayeroff), and honesty and noble lie (theories of Carr/ Ellin/ Bok). In conclusion, the teacher ended the lesson with a class vote, the result was the class will choose not to tell CIE the truth but to keep quiet and translate the. Documents.

References

Bek, L. (1994). *Reclaiming educational administration as a caring profession* (pp. 5-20). New York: Teachers College Press.

Bok, S. (1978). Lies for the public good. In J. C. Callahan (ed.) (1988). *Ethical Issues in Professional Life* (pp. 150-156). New York: Oxford University Press.

Callahan, J. C. (1988). *Ethical issues in professional life*. New York: Oxford University Press.

Carr, A. Z. (1968). *Is business bluffing ethical?*. Boston: Harvard University Graduate School of Business Administration.

Ellin, J. S. (1982). Special professional morality and the duty of veracity. In J. C. Callahan (ed.) (1988). *Ethical Issues in Professional Life* (pp. 130-139). New York: Oxford University Press.

Galligan, C. (1987). Moral Orientation and Moral Development. In E. F. Kittay & D. T. Meyers (Eds.), *Women and moral theory* (pp. 19-33). Totawa, NJ: Rowman & Littlefield Publishers.

Lee, H. (1960). *To kill a mockingbird*. New York : Warner Books.

Mayeroff, M. (1995). On caring. In Williams. C. (ed.) (1995). *On Love and Friendship* (pp. 335-355). Boston: Jones and Bartlett Publishers.

Ethical Dilemmas

Chapter 3

Church Planting Problems

by David Thorne
Cleveland, Ohio

Definitions:
Church Plant: A church being started from nothing

Lead Church Planter: Person leading the start of the new church

Church Management Team: Representative of financially invested churches dedicated to helping lead church planter begin the church well

Church Planter Assessment: Weekend-long assessment process a lead church planter goes through before being allowed to plant a church

Launch: Refers to the date of the first public worship service of the new church

Launch Team: Group of individuals dedicated to helping "launch" or start a new church

Characters:
Derek: Main character

Marcus: Lead church planter

Jarvis: Wise pastor from whom Derek seeks advice

Church Planting Problems

Derek knew the management team needed to make a decision, but there seemed to be no good answers. He took a deep breath and purposefully made eye contact with the other three men at the table. The question *what should we do* hung heavy in the air, like an anvil high above their heads, held only by a string.

Like him, they represented churches financially invested in starting Marcus' new church plant. As a management team, the men understood it was their responsibility to represent their churches and oversee the planting of this new church. But, something *had* to be done and Derek knew their decision would have consequences.

Marcus also sat at the table, waiting for answers. It was June and his church was scheduled to open in September, only a few short months away. In many ways he was prepared. He had a small, but devoted launch team of about twenty hopeful volunteers committed to helping launch the new church. Marcus had also signed a contract to hold Sunday services in a local movie theater and had purchased most of the equipment necessary to do so. Church services in a movie theater may seem unconventional, but when you're hoping to attract those who don't typically attend church, creative ideas like this are important.

This creativity extended into a young worship pastor named Eric, whom Marcus had invited to help start the church. Eric had agreed to raise his own salary to help the church get started and was set to arrive in the next few weeks. Everything was going great except for one major area- finances.

Financial Frustrations

Marcus was set to run out of money in early December, nearly two months after opening. He had quit his previous job as an associate pastor to plant this church and he had no idea what he would do if his church failed.

Marcus took a deep breath as his eyes passed over the other men at the table. He was thankful for each one and the investment in time, energy, and money they were making to his young church. But, their investment made up about one half of what he needed for the first year of his church plant. He was supposed to fundraise the rest. Marcus tried, but he struggled to raise the money needed. Now, with only a few months to go, his church felt like the Titanic barreling towards a financial iceberg.

Deeper Issues

Derek knew money was a big issue for Marcus' young church, but the problems went deeper. He thought back to the most recent management team meeting where Marcus shared an updated vision for his new church and practiced the sermon he was preparing to give on opening Sunday. It was not good. His sermon, like his vision, was messy and unconvincing. A church plant with no money and a pastor with no plan, who couldn't preach effectively, would not last long.

It seemed unfair to push forward with launching a church plant doomed to failure. Derek liked Marcus a lot, but questioned how he even made it this far in his process. Marcus had approached a national church planting organization about a year ago, expressing interest in church planting.

The organization put Marcus through an extensive assessment process to determine if leading a church plant would be a good fit. Marcus passed the assessment and was connected with a group of churches that would become his management team. The church planting organization helped coach Marcus and directed the management team along the way. But, their guidance only went so far, Derek and his team had to decide what they could or should do next.

No Good Answers

Derek was frustrated with the entire situation- how could experts in church planting assessment spend multiple days investigating Marcus' ability to successfully plant a church and miss gaps in essential pastoral abilities? Marcus had a great personality and an infectious smile, but was clearly missing skills necessary for a successful church plant.

Derek felt like his management team had been given an old car with a rusty engine and encouraged to go win a race. With sufficient time it may be possible to get the car running adequately, but winning seemed far from reasonable.

But, none of that mattered now. Marcus had developed a small, devoted group of volunteers ready to start a church. Marcus had everything set to go, including a worship pastor. The only thing he didn't have was money, or the management team's confidence that this plant would end in anything but failure.

The management team had to decide- do we put off the church launch, giving Marcus time to raise more money or push ahead as planned and hope for the best? There was also an option to shut down the church now. If the church was destined to fail anyways not paying Marcus' salary for the next few months would save the investing churches money. Every decision had a downside. Soon silence enveloped the small table as options and factors and disappointment swirled around like an invisible, insidious cyclone. Any decision would unleash the twisting, twirling wind, leaving a wake of potential destruction.

One of the other management team members broke the sullen silence by suggesting they take a break and meet again in a few days to make a final decision. Coffee cups were long-empty and the popular lunch destination was quickly filling with hungry patrons for lunch. Derek said good-bye to the other pastors and made his way to the front door.

Taking a Break

Exiting the restaurant's front door the summer heat felt heavy, weighing on his body like the pressure of the decision the management team needed to make. The bright white sun shone down like a spotlight, following Derek as he walked toward his car. He began to sweat under its unflinching warm gaze. He unlocked the car, slid into the driver seat, and quickly turned on the engine to get the air-conditioning going.

As Derek waited for the car to cool, options danced in Derek's head. He felt like every decision could lead to calamity and disappointment. It made him think of the sarcastic customer service sign he recently saw on a friend's work desk that read, "I can only please one person per day. Today's not your day and tomorrow doesn't look too good either." This made Derek smile, even though he knew the reality of displeasing people was not very funny.

Derek zeroed back in on his present predicament and the face of his long-time mentor Jarvis came to mind. Jarvis was one of the wisest men and best pastors Derek knew. Whenever he felt stuck in some church problem he'd always call Jarvis, who always seemed to have pertinent wisdom to share. Derek knew the first thing Jarvis would encourage him to do is to weigh his options.

Weighing the Options

Jarvis grew up on a small farm in the country and in thinking through this situation Derek could almost hear Jarvis say, "There's more than one way to get milk from a cow." Although Derek had always wondered if there really was more than one way to get milk from a cow, he understood Jarvis' point. Jarvis believed problems must be considered from different perspectives. This was especially important when decisions involved people. It was essential to slow down and truly attempt to view problems from other points of view.

When it came to Marcus' church there seemed to be three main options: close the church now, let the church launch as planned, or postpone the launch of the church. Derek figured his best bet would be to think through each option, considering the possible consequences of each choice.

Option 1: Closing the Church Now

Closing the church now seemed to be the most extreme option. But, based on Marcus' present financial prognosis, he was quickly draining his remaining resources. On top of this, the management team did not believe Marcus had the skills necessary to succeed. These two factors encouraged closing the church as a viable option with a few benefits.

The biggest benefit was saving money. If the management team made the decision to close the church plant now, it would save $20,000-$30,000. This would include Marcus' salary, money set aside for advertising, rent, and other last minute church purchases. If the church was going to close anyway, it would be nice to have a portion of the money invested in this church plant back to reinvest in a future church plant. This seemed like a wise use of money.

This thought brought to mind the time Derek grappled with firing a flailing staff member only to have Jarvis declare, "Sometimes the most caring option is to put a sick animal out of his misery." He followed this enigmatic and morose statement with a story about a beloved family horse who became ill in its old age.

When talking about the best course of action, his family realized they were keeping the horse alive because they didn't want to let it go. It was not because it was in the best interest of the elderly, sick animal. The poor horse was in pain and they came to the conclusion the most loving thing they could do was allow it to pass on in peace.

Jarvis' story helped Derek fire his struggling staff and he wondered if the story would apply here as well. If this church is destined to die, then could the most compassionate choice be "putting it out of its misery"? Similar to Jarvis' family farm, are members of the management team keeping the sick church alive because making the choice to pull the plug seems too painful? It's entirely possible. But, there is one other benefit to closing the church now- volunteers.

Marcus had gathered about fifteen people committed to help launch his new church. As the church moved towards its first Sunday, each launch team member would be giving a lot of time and energy. Beginning a new church can be exhausting. As a new church starts, volunteers have to wear many hats. The issue is, the more time and energy volunteers give to a new church, the more invested they become in the church's success. The more invested a volunteer is in the church's success, the more it will hurt if the church were forced to close. If the church is destined to close, then the sooner this happens the less it will impact and affect volunteers.

Derek thought of an analogy with dating. He imagined a guy and girl beginning to date. But, after a few dates the girl knows the relationship isn't going anywhere. The girl could quit the relationship then, or do nothing and wait a few months until the guy comes to the same conclusion.

The issue is, the longer the couple waits to break up, the harder it will be. The wisest course of action would probably be for the girl to break up with the guy as soon as she realizes the relationship will not last. Similarly, if Marcus' church was doomed to close, then the sooner the management team makes the decision to close, the less hurt volunteers will experience.

The major downside to closing the church now was the chance that Marcus could succeed. There is a chance the church could get off to a great start and grow quickly. It was *possible* for Marcus to raise the money necessary to sustain him through is first year of ministry. Neither was very likely, but if the management team closed the church now they'd never find out.

It would be tough for Marcus and his volunteers to always wonder if his church might have succeeded if given the chance. Maybe Marcus and his team deserved the opportunity to try. This thought led Derek to ponder the second major option the management team could make: letting the church launch as planned.

Option 2: Let the Church Launch as Planned

The management team could do nothing and let the entire scenario play out naturally. Marcus' church would either grow quickly, or completely run out of money within the first two months.

There were a few benefits to this plan. The major benefit would be letting Marcus and his team find out if the church could succeed. Yes, Marcus and his volunteers would risk the pain of their beloved church running out of money, but they would never have to wonder what *could* have happened if given the opportunity to start the church.

Derek's mind wandered back to the fall of his senior year of high school. He was on the cross country team at the time, though placing high in any race seemed laughable. One day the gym teacher saw Derek run and begged him to join the football team immediately. Due to the commitment he had made to the cross-country team, Derek declined. But, even now, he wonders what it would have been like to play football his senior year. It may be silly, but Derek thought about this missed opportunity every once in a while.

Planting a church is a much bigger deal than high school football. Was the management sufficiently convinced the church would fail that they should take the opportunity for success away from Marcus and his team? As Derek walked near the restaurant, he wished he could see the future. Besides winning the lottery and buying his wife a pool, he would definitely find out if Marcus' church would succeed. Unfortunately, Derek could not see the future.

The main downside to this option was very similar to closing the church immediately. The more Marcus and his team invested in the church before closing, the more emotional pain they could experience when it closed. The only difference is disappointment from the church closure would extend beyond Marcus and his team. New people would attend Marcus' church after launch and each would experience loss if it closed.

There was also the issue of money. If the church was allowed to use all its resources until there were none left- then there would be none left. This means the money Derek's church committed to planting this new church would be entirely used up.

Derek would have to explain to his church what happened and he might have to defend his decision to invest in this church plant to a few key leaders. If the church ran out of money in this scenario, then the management team would be left to handle leftover equipment and disappointed people. This didn't sound like fun to Derek.

Option 3: Postpone the Launch of the Church

There was one final option- to postpone the launch of the church. The main benefit of this option was to give Marcus time to raise more money and find additional launch team members. But, there was a big downside to this option. There would be no guarantee Marcus would raise more money or find new launch team members. Also, if the church launch was postponed three months, Marcus would still need to be paid during that time period. This would mean the church would still be losing money, but without the chance to raise new money from collecting offerings on Sunday morning. This option could result in speeding up the resource depletion.

Calling a Friend

Speaking of resource depletion, Derek realized he'd been sitting in a running car for a while. By now the car was cool, almost cold, so Derek made his way home. Derek's family helped take his mind off Marcus' church that evening, but the impending decision was always present, lurking in the back of his mind. Derek didn't sleep very well that night. He kept going over the three options in his head and had no idea how to figure out which one was best.

In the morning Derek groggily made his way to the kitchen to find the largest cup he could for coffee. He briefly eyed one of his kids' sports water jugs thinking it seemed to be an appropriate size for the job. Derek settled for a normal-sized coffee cup, filled it with coffee and slowly made his way to the kitchen table. As he sat down to drink his coffee he noticed his wife watching him.

"I'm sorry you had trouble sleeping last night," she said.

"Thanks."

"Umm, could I make a suggestion?" she said sheepishly.

Derek wasn't so sure about what his wife was going to say next but cautiously replied, "Ok."

"Why don't you give Jarvis a call today and talk about the situation with Marcus' church?"

His wife's words hit him like the cold spray from a garden hose and he suddenly felt awake. That was a wonderful idea. Derek thanked his wife and ran upstairs to get ready for the day. Before long he was out the door and in his church office dialing his mentor. "Hello," Jarvis answered. Derek exchanged pleasantries and then launched into the issues with Marcus' church plant. He explained the three options before the management team and asked for Jarvis' help to decide which option presented the best solution.

Two Principles

Jarvis always appreciated a call from Derek. He loved Derek's enthusiasm, though sometimes thought he took himself too seriously. Jarvis appreciated the complications within Derek's scenario and it brought to mind something he learned long ago on the farm. "When it comes to dropping an egg, how you do it doesn't matter- it will still crack," Jarvis shared.

Responding to the silence on the other end of the phone, Jarvis went on to explain, "Derek, complicated questions often have complicated answers and sometimes there's no perfect answer." As a pastor, Jarvis has had to make many complicated decisions throughout the years. He had always felt there were two main values that could direct decisions: a principle of benefit maximization and a principle of equal respect.

The principle of benefit maximization encourages decisions that create the most benefit for the most people. This viewpoint values the consequences of every action and looks to find the decision that results in the most favorable outcome.

On the other hand, the principle of equal respect emphasizes the people involved in the decision. The goal of this principle is to treat each person with the same respect that we would want to receive. It emphasizes the welfare of all individuals involved in the situation. Jarvis explained these two principles to Derek and asked him to talk through each for his situation.

Principle of Benefit Maximization

Once more, Derek was in awe of Jarvis' insight, and a little confused by his analogies. But, he figured thinking through his situation with these two principles in mind could be helpful. The principle of benefit maximization seemed interesting because there were many potential consequences to the management team's decision.

If the management team decided to close the church now, this would save money for the four investing churches. This money could then be used to invest in other, more promising church plants that could eventually help hundreds or even thousands of people. If the management team felt sure that Marcus' church would fail, then saving their money and reinvesting it in future church plants seemed to have the greatest benefit for the most people.

But, the benefit of this choice rests on the word "if". *If* the management team believes that Marcus will fail, then this it is a good idea to close. The question is, what percentage does the management team give Marcus to fail as a church planter? Do they believe his church has a 60% chance to fail? Would they place his chance for failure even higher- maybe 85%? Or, would they deem his chances of failure at 50% or lower?

The answer to this question could affect the consequences. If the management teams believes there is less than a 50% chance that Marcus' church could fail, then allowing the church to launch as planned to produce the greatest consequences.

Derek and the other management team members already have a lot of time, energy, and money invested in Marcus. Each of their churches had already budgeted money for this purpose. It is hard to say what would happen if each church took their money back now. There is a chance some churches would not reallocate their money to a new church plant. But, each church was made their own decisions in this matter and some church leadership boards may be less inclined to jump into another church plant after one failed. There is also a chance their group would not find another planter for a few years.

If Marcus' church succeeds, then it would have the greatest chance for immediate impact. There would be a church where that was not one before. There could be hundreds of people hearing about God's love for the first time. The potential of church plant success could create very positive consequences.

There is also the good will a church plant success would create in each of the investing churches. Each congregation would be excited about church planting. This could lead to more money allocated to church planting in the future. The success of Marcus' church lays seed that could produce the fruit of future financial investment in more church plants. But, in each of these options, the most important feature is the percentage the management team would give Marcus' church for forced closure due to lack of finances. If Derek and his team were going to use this principle to determine what to do, they will need to discuss what percent chance they give Marcus's church to succeed.

Principle of Equal Respect

The principle of equal respect, on the other hand, considers the people involved in the situation. The first thing Derek wanted to consider was how he would be feeling if he were in a similar situation as Marcus. He imagined himself being a few months out from the launch of his church plant. He had left his previous job for this opportunity. He had been working long hours and lost sleep, and spent tons of time on the phone, all for the chance to tell people about God's love.

Derek knew he would be terrified of failure, but with only a few months out he had to find out if this church plant would work. If the church plant was never given the opportunity to succeed, he would always wonder what *could have been*. If the plant would fail, then Derek would at least know he gave it his best shot. If Derek was in Marcus' position, there would be no question what decision he would hope the management team would make. Derek would clearly want the chance to launch the church.

The principle of equal respect changes the paradigm for church plant investment. The principle of benefit maximization would encourage a church to invest in a successful church. But, the principle of equal respect focuses a church on the actual planter.

Once a church planter is identified, then the management team's job is to help that specific planter launch their church. The investment is less about success and more about preparing that pastor for their first Sunday. This principle of equal respect asks investing churches to focus more on the journey towards launch than the outcome.

This principle prioritizes relationship and care for the individuals involved. If one viewed this scenario through a lens of care and asked the question, "What does our relationship require," then the path forward seems clear. Allowing the church to launch on schedule seems like the most caring option. It would definitely be what Marcus would want. But, having said that, there is one other way to view the most caring option.

If the plant management team knew the plant would fail, then it could be argued the most loving thing to do would be to close it down before it failed. Derek imagined a mom or dad trying to convince their three year old that touching a hot stove is not a good idea, but giving them the option to touch it or not. Clearly, loving parents should not leave the choice of whether or not to touch a hot stove to a three-year-old. Children this age do not have the mental faculties necessary to make a wise decision. Was this a similar scenario? If this church is doomed to failure, then wouldn't closing it now be the most caring thing to do?

Closing the church now could save Marcus from unnecessary pain and loss. It could also protect his launch team from similar feelings of loss. Everyone would still experience disappointment, but to a lesser degree. If the church felt confident the church plant would fail, then this could be the most caring option.

The question here could come back to what percent sure the management team would be that Marcus' church would fail. The difference between asking the question with principle of equal respect in mind versus the principle of benefit maximization is in the level of percent. Because relationships are prioritized in this principle, then the management team would likely need to be 90-95% Marcus' church would fail before deciding to pull the plug. Anything less than that and Derek knew his relationship with Marcus would dictate giving him a chance to succeed- or fail.

Percentage Wisdom

"Well?" Jarvis asked aloud. Derek shook his head slightly to refocus attention on his mentor on the other end of the phone. He had finished talking through all the options using the principles of benefit maximization and equal respect and realized he had fallen silent, contemplating new information. "What percentage would you give Marcus for failure?" Jarvis asked. Derek realized his answer to this question would help determine the management team's best course of action. "I don't know right now," Derek answered, unsettled. Jarvis encouraged Derek to sleep on his decision, and then after sharing one more offbeat analogy involving farm animals, the two hung up.

As Derek hung up his call with Jarvis, he felt the familiar weight of the management team's decision return. But, Derek didn't feel helpless. He knew the question he needed to answer and the factors involved in making a wise decision.

The Decision

Derek woke up Saturday morning nervous, but ready. His conversation with Jarvis had been helpful and Derek felt prepared to make a decision. As he drove to the familiar coffee shop, he prayed everyone on the management team would agree on the best course of action. He walked in and found round table in a cozy corner of the restaurant. Soon, the other members of the management team and Marcus arrived.

The small group greeted each other warmly, but conversation soon turned to answering the question on the table: what to do with Marcus' church plant. The management team had decided to meet together for an hour before Marcus joined them, so Derek knew their time to discuss was precious.

Derek jumped in and asked if he could briefly share some insights from his conversation with Jarvis. The group seemed glad to put off making a decision for a few more minutes. Derek quickly walked the group through the principle of benefit maximization and equal respect. He ended with the question, "what percent do we give Marcus' church for survival?"

This was obviously an awkward, though necessary question. The team cautiously and fairly quickly came to a conclusion. As a group they gave Marcus between a 40-60% chance for failure. Using both the principle of benefit maximization and equal respect, it seemed like allowing Marcus the chance to plant his church was the best option. On top of this, the group agreed the principle of equal respect weighed more in their decision than optimal consequences. They acknowledged the most salient feature in this scenario was their relationship to Marcus and his opportunity to plant a church. Their relationship with Marcus required that they give him the opportunity to launch his church. They agreed their ultimate responsibility was to do everything in their power to help Marcus launch. Derek wholeheartedly agreed with each decision.

Having decided the management team was able to turn their attention to helping Marcus launch as effectively as possible. Time was short and there was still a lot of work to do. Derek hoped every church launch wouldn't be this complicated and he still had no idea of Marcus' church would succeed, but he felt confident in the team's decision. Soon, the management team could see Marcus entering the restaurant and making his way toward the group. Time would tell is the management team was making the right decision.

Chapter 4

Office Dalliances

by Emmah M. Muema
Kenya, East Africa

Ethical Dilemmas

Definitions:
Sexual harassment: Overt or implied, unwanted sexual advances or remarks

Kshs: Kenyan Shilling, 1 U.S. dollar equals about 100 Kenyan Shillings

Banking Director: Position in a Kenyan bank similar to a branch manager in the American system

Characters:
Charles Osborn: Director of business at a commercial bank in Kenya

Maggie: Relationship officer in the business department of Charles Osborn

Danny: Human Resource Manager for the bank

Office Dalliances

Sexual harassment happens everywhere and in every industry. For years the banking sector in Kenya was full of blatant sexual harassment. But, most cases were never reported for fear of losing employment or facing public humiliation. As a new generation has entered the workforce, there has been a shift with a higher number of reported cases and overall increased awareness of these common workplace issues. But, sometimes sexual harassment cases are more complicated than they originally seem.

Kenyan Bank Overview

In 2018, there were forty-five banks in Kenya, including both local and international brands. The country's currency at the time was the Kenyan shilling (Kshs.). One shilling was equivalent to one hundred United States dollars (USD).

Kenya's banking industry is prestigious and filled with highly paid employees. The industry is highly regulated by the Central Bank of Kenya and several international bodies in its operations. Human resource policies differ from bank to bank, but generally align with international and local labor laws, and the 2010 Constitution of Kenya.

Until the early 2000's, employees were hired at the clerical level without bachelor's degrees and proceeded to acquire these credentials while in employment. The ability for job advancement endeared many young and ambitious Kenyans to the sector. However, the power to oversee career advancement created opportunities for unethical behavior by some banking directors. But, after investigating the context, the victim may not always be as innocent as they seem.

Unethical Opportunities

Charles Osborn works for Upendo Commercial bank (UCB) in Kenya. He is the director in charge of business with a large work force under him of sales men and women. Maggie is a young promising relationship officer working in the business department, under Charles's team.

In January 2015, Maggie approached Charles with a request to borrow Kshs. 100,000 (US $1,000) with a promise to pay it back within two months. Charles had been secretly admiring Maggie and so he took the opportunity to ask her for a sexual favor as he advanced her the cash.

It is not clear whether Charles requested for the sexual favor before giving Maggie the cash or after. Charles withdrew cash from a private account unknown to his wife and wired the money to Maggie. The two then made arrangements to meet in a private hotel room.

The next day Charles arrived at the hotel and entered the rented room. Before moving any further, Charles excused himself to use the restroom. While Charles was away Maggie quickly and quietly installed a small camera to record their dalliance.

Human Resource Involvement

Two months after the escapade, Charles began demanding his payment for the borrowed money. Maggie had yet to repay any money. So, Charles decided to lodge a complaint with human resources (HR) to put pressure on Maggie to repay the cash. In his complaint, Charles claimed that Maggie had refused to pay back the borrowed money.

Maggie was summoned by HR to explain why she had not made any payments on her loan from the business director. In her defense, Maggie played the video she recorded from the hotel and alleged that Charles gave her the money in payment for the sexual favor. Shocked by the twist of the events, the HR Director, Danny Ochieng and his team requested Maggie to keep the matter quiet until they determined what to do next.

Unfortunately, HR had summoned Maggie through an intimidating memo that stated in part to "… show cause why disciplinary action should not be taken against you…" These notes are typically placed in an employee's file, making the matter "official".

Facts of the Case

Analyzing the case requires a good understanding of the facts. These are summarized below:

1. Charles interaction with his subordinate is irregular. Bosses do not normally "lend" their subordinates their personal money.

2. Charles Osborn is a disgruntled business director at UCB, a senior employee in the bank who advanced Kshs. 100,000 to Maggie his subordinate under unclear terms.

3. Charles lodged an official non-payment complaint with HR against Maggie for lack of repayment.

4. Maggie and Charles engaged in a sexual encounter which Maggie, recorded on video. This proves the incident occurred. Maggie claims she fully paid the debt in kind to Charles.

5. UCB human resources policy section 8 addresses employee code of conduct and ethical behavior. Section 8.1.6 addresses grievance handling, while section 8.2.11 addresses sexual harassment.

The above facts raise several dilemma questions for human resources to resolve. These are:

1. Was the Kshs. 100,000 a loan to Maggie or a payment for the sexual favor?

2. What does Maggie's claim that the money was a payment for sex mean?

   a. Was she practicing prostitution? Or;

   b. Did she intend to blackmail Charles by claiming the money was advanced for sex?

   c. Was Charles paying for the sex or is he being blackmailed?

3. What motivated Charles to advance cash to a junior employee in his team?

4. Is Maggie honest in claiming that the cash was advanced as payment for sex?

5. Was Charles aware that his action of giving Maggie the Kshs. 100,000 may have been

perpetuating prostitution, which is an illegal practice in Kenya?

6. Bank policy states that its employees should not "live beyond their means". Does borrowing an amount she is unable to pay (Ksh. 100,000) mean she is living beyond her means?

7. Should we assume that the sexual encounter was consensual because until Charles demanded repayment of the cash advance, Maggie had not filed any complaint?

8. Why was it necessary for Maggie to record the encounter? Is it possible she planned to set up Charles?

9. Is Maggie aware that claiming the cash advance was payment for sex implies she was engaging in prostitution?

HR Complications

According to the Bank financial conduct policy, staff are not permitted to borrow money they cannot repay as this is construed as 'living beyond one's means'. This policy in the banking sector in Kenya is enforced as a mechanism of monitoring staff lifestyle due to frequent misappropriation of funds by bank employees. Violating this policy is a serious offense that can lead to termination.

In this case, when Charles reported the matter to HR, he was aware this clause would intimidate Maggie to pay back the advanced cash. However, the hotel tryst adds a substantial twist for HR policy enforcement. Can they enforce repayment with the new details to the case? How do they discipline Charles, noting that his complaint implicates him in a possible prostitution situation? Did Charles engage in sexual harassment of a junior staff or was it a consensual encounter? If consensual, does HR apply the sexual harassment policy to Charles?

As a junior staff, Maggie is a member of the bankers' union, therefore if the matter is escalated to the union, things may get complicated quickly. What policies apply for or against Maggie as an employee? Should Charles be paid back his money?

Carefully Implementing Policy

HR director Danny recognizes he must take the lead in handling this case for various reasons. First, HR is the custodian of staff policies and its enforcement. Second, the case involves his peer and the entire workforce will be waiting with bated breath to see whether Maggie will be treated fairly. Danny knew he needed to handle this case carefully.

The official procedure requires Danny to appoint a disciplinary committee (DC) as stipulated by the HR manual. His first dilemma is the composition of the committee, because DC members are typically HR, and one's immediate supervisor. But, due to the sensitivity of this situation Danny chose to include a legal officer and a director from an unrelated division.

The committee reviewed the facts and noted that the complainant in this case is Charles, who claims he lent Maggie Kshs.100,000 which she has refused to pay back. In order to be fair to Charles, they began their review using the personal finance policy.

The committee noted that Maggie had not lodged a sexual harassment charge against Charles, therefore they proceeded with the hearing under the financial misconduct concern. But, they also considered the bank's sexual harassment policy. It was provided to all DC members in readiness for the hearing and states:

> "An employee is sexually harassed if a colleague, (a) directly or indirectly requests that employee for sexual intercourse, sexual contact or any other form of sexual activity that contains and implied or expressed as: (i) promise of preferential treatment in employment;(ii) Threat of detrimental treatment in employment; or(iii) Threat about the present or future employment status of the employee; (b) Uses language whether written or spoken of a sexual nature; (c) Uses visual material of a sexual nature; or (d) shows physical behavior of a sexual nature which directly or indirectly subjects the employee to behavior that is unwelcome or offensive to that employee and that by its nature has a detrimental effect on that employee's

employment, job performance, or job satisfaction."

Upon review of the policy the committee notes Charles appears not to have violated any of the described clauses. It was then time to hear directly from both parties in order to determine what the disciplinary committee should decide.

Maggie's Testimony

Maggie arrived for the hearing and was sat at a round table with the DC members. In her defense, Maggie told the committee that she had a cordial relationship with her boss, and that the whole issue started one January evening when she worked late. That evening she was pondering how she was going to make ends meet to payday. She told the DC that Charles normally walks round the offices in the evening to check and engage with staff working late.

On that fateful Tuesday evening, Charles walked into the office from a regular management meeting at around 6.30 pm and found Maggie at her desk. He picked a conversation with her on work related matters then the issue of January being a long month and having overspent during the holidays found its way into their conversation. Somehow Charles offered to "assist" Maggie "survive" the month by advancing her Kshs. 100,000.

Charles promised to give Maggie the cash within 2 working days. But during the two days as she waited for the cash, Charles would stop at her desk to compliment her dressing and on one of the days, he asked her for a sex. She received the cash 48 hours after their initial conversation, but by the end of that week Charles had pursued the sex issue and she accepted.

In Maggie's understanding, having sex with Charles was repayment for the cash advanced to her. She therefore did not understand why Charles was asking for double payment. When the committee asked why she recorded their social meeting, she said that knowing Charles was a born-again Christian, she was afraid he would deny the encounter or force her to repay the funds. She also felt that, as the boss, HR may believe his story more than hers, so she wanted to have proof of the encounter.

She told the committee that she did not file a complaint because as far as she was concerned, they both got what they wanted, she needed cash and Charles wanted sex, but when she got the memo on disciplinary action, she got upset and that is why she produced the evidence. The committee informed Maggie that her admitting receiving payment for sex is prostitution, which is illegal according to section 153 and 154 of the Penal Code.

Maggie pleaded with the committee that she needed the money to pay school fees for her son who had been unable to go to school for three weeks of the first term because she did not have money to pay school fees. She pleaded that she was unable to repay Charles the cash, but she believes Charles received fair payment for his cash. She requested the committee not to pursue the issue further and promised she would not engage in future prostitution.

Charles' Defense

In his defense, Charles claimed that he found Maggie in the office crying at around 6.30 pm and when he enquired what the matter was, she explained that she did not have school fees for her son. She asked Charles to advance her Kshs. 100,000, and promised to refund the money at the end of February. When asked about the sexual escapade, Charles claimed that it was the work of the devil and he does not recollect what or how he found himself in that position.

Committee Deliberations

The committee advised him that according to Maggie, the debt was paid when she accepted to have sex with him. The committee further pointed out that by paying for sex, Charles was aiding prostitution which is illegal.

Charles categorically denied any involvement in prostitution as he was not aware Maggie had decided to take the money as payment for sex. He further stated that he did not sexually harass Maggie, but she willingly accepted his cash and advances- explaining why she had not filed any complaint against him. He blamed the devil for his weak moments and regrets the outcome. After the hearing, the committee summarized the issues as follows:

1. Charles was unaware of Maggie's intentions of using the cash advanced to her as payment for sex.

2. Charles involvement in sex with a junior staff is unacceptable however, according to the bank policy, there is no violation on his part.

3. Charles would like Maggie to refund the cash.

4. Maggie had no intention of repaying the loan, debt is already paid.

5. Maggie's decision to exchange sex for the cash loan amounts to prostitution. However, since her partner was not aware of her intentions, does this still amount to prostitution?

6. The committee has to decide whether to escalate Maggie's actions of prostitution.

The committee recognized that the sexual harassment policy is not sufficiently comprehensive to address the case at hand. The HR director recognized that his role is critical in guiding the committee in their decision especially on ethical and moral matters.

In the ethic of justice, Danny argues Charles deserves a refund of the loan amount advanced to Maggie, despite his error in judgement, quoting Aristotle (350) that it is presumed those who act unjustly have too much and the person unjustly treated has too little, which is not the case before them.

He argued that Maggie changed the rules of the game midstream which was unfair for Charles, who did not have an opportunity to accept the modified terms of engagement. Other committee members felt, if repayment is enforced, it should mean double repayment on Maggie's part. The maximum principal in the concept of equality requires that inequalities are to be permitted only when everyone benefits.

Sam, the legal officer, reminded the committee that all exchanges must be comparable in value. Therefore, if the committee ruled in favor of Charles it would be unfair to Maggie, since she would suffer from the same incident twice.

One HR member on the committee wondered whether Maggie voluntarily chose to be treated unjustly since not all unjust actions are involuntary (Callahan, 1988). This member was alluding to Maggie putting herself in a "disadvantaged situation", to access intrinsic value and gain from the transaction.

Other members were of the opinion that Charles did not deserve to be paid because as the senior, he should not have engaged in personal matters with his junior colleague. Overall, DC members advocated for Charles dismissal from the bank. Unfortunately, there was no single policy violation the DC could use to warrant employee termination.

On the other hand, some DC members were of the opinion, Maggie was calculating and took advantage of her boss. In changing the rules of the game, Maggie was in control and manipulated the entire situation. This is affirmed by Starratt, (1991) when he alludes to the fact that an individual will enter into a social relation to advance their own advantage.

This is true for Charles, who is driven by his personal interest and passion. The relationship these two entered into was essentially artificial and governed by self-interest (Starratt, 1991). A libertarian would argue both Maggie and Charles received maximum value and maximized on the transaction, each gaining intrinsic value, Maggie's son went to school and Charles's passion was quenched (Howe, 1991).

Guided by these arguments, committee members were of the opinion both Charles and Maggie received payment for the interests that guided them to enter into the relationship and therefore the committee proposed to issue both with strongly worded warning letters. The warning letters will serve as a reprimand for both Charles and Maggie against ever getting involved in a similar incident. They came to this decision on a

Friday and planned to share their decision with Maggie and Charles on Monday.

News Travels Fast

Those working in the bank awoke on Monday morning to a shocking headline. A " junior female staff" was suing an unnamed managing director for sexual harassment. In addition to having details of the case, the newspaper article contained facts on Charles and Maggie's specific situation. Their article compromised the disciplinary committee's decision made only a few days earlier. The disciplinary committee met promptly to discuss the news but weren't ready to share their verdict. Instead, they decided to revisit some facts of the case.

Policy Problems

The legal officer noted that the world would be watching how the bank handled Maggie's admission to prostitution. Danny drew the committee to the arguments of Aristotle (350 B.C.) on "unjust" acts that are contrary to the law, both of which support Charles and Maggie. Maggie committed adultery for the sake of gain and made money by it, while Charles did the same at the bidding of appetite though he lost money and was penalized for it.

The latter is self-indulgent, and the former is unjust, meaning Maggie broke the law. To prosecute Maggie means Charles must also be connected to the case. Yet lending money to Maggie to pay fees for her son was an act of caring. Would it be fair to drag Charles into a suit that he was unaware of?

The HR policy on sexual harassment is drafted with the male as the aggressor. In the ethic of critique, the structured bias of the policy fails to protect Charles and other male employees, who may fall victim of sexual harassment. The committee, in its final deliberation, is drawn to the ethic of critique which recognizes biases in policies and law. It is urged to be fair, noting if there is injustice in their ruling it will affect Charles and Maggie but will indirectly affect all UCB employees.

The committee upheld its earlier decision to issue warning letters and closed the matter. The consequence of this decision is that HR may be viewed as weak in making tough calls where Directors are involved. The ruling may be seen as setting a precedence that the leadership will condone illegal behavior, a serious outcome of the ruling especially if learned friends choose to sue board members and directors.

HR needs to make firm decisions that not only resonate with the internal policy but reflect the rules and views of society from the legal instruments. But then leaders of institutions are drawn from the same society, presenting a double-edged sword.

The Final Verdict

After reviewing submissions by both Charles and Maggie, DC members voted to immediately terminate the services of both Charles and Maggie and forward the prostitution case to the government prosecutor. DC members were of the opinion that the UCB brand should not be associated with unlawful behavior or transactions at any time and that the espoused behavior by both

Charles and Maggie did not fit into the institution values as stipulated in the manual.

The values require staff to treat each other with respect and to uphold integrity. Further the code of conduct of employees was violated when Charles sought sexual favors from his junior staff and Maggie's acceptance of these advances in addition to admitting that she chose to repay the loan using sex was a disgrace to the institution.

The DC was disgusted by Maggie's recording, a clear indication that there was lack of integrity and self-respect. The drastic decision was made by DC members fully aware the Maggie is a union employee and that the union may seek her reinstatement.

Quoting the 2010 constitution chapter 6 and 10 guides on matters of integrity and leadership of institutions, while the public officers code of conduct and ethics guides on behavior and officers conduct. Termination letters were issued for both Charles and Maggie and the prostitution case was forwarded to the public prosecutor.

Conclusion

In reviewing literature, as early as 350 B.C. similar issues were addressed whether in the work place or among society. Aristotle argues for and against the unjust, unprivileged and privileged by harmonizing those who gain and lose, stating why money was introduced in society as a standard measure of value. Connecting the writings of Aristotle, the ethic of critique demonstrates that institutional policies are crafted with obvious human biases. The ethic of justice, on the other hand, considers fairness relative to the situation, balancing the needs of both the individual and society. It is evident, therefore, that the ethic of care in our relationships is reduced to human interpretations and governing ourselves becomes a thin balance for leaders. Leaders not only judge right from wrong, balance winners and losers, fairly and unfairly treated, individual benefits verses society, the ultimate decision is held in the hands of the beholders perception.

References

Callahan, J. C. (1988). *Ethical issues in professional life*. New York: Oxford University Press.

Howe, K. R. (1993). The liberal democratic tradition and educational ethics. In Strike & Ternasky (eds.), *Ethics for Professionals in Education* (Chapter 2, pp. 27-42)

Starratt, R. J. (1991). Building an ethical School: A theory for practice in educational leadership. *Educational Administration Quarterly*, 27(2), 185-202

Chapter 5

The Good and the Bad Cop

By Oluwatobi Taiwo Ishola
Nigeria, West Africa

Ethical Dilemmas

Definitions:
Patrol partners: Two police officers assigned to work on a shift together in a patrol car

Homicide: Deliberate killing of another person

Whistle blowing: When a person informs authorities of illicit activities within an organization

Characters:
Officer Samantha Wosilak: patrol partner of Officer Joe Sanie in the Greensnake Police Department

Officer Joe Sanie: patrol partner of Officer Samantha Wosilak in the Greensnake Police Department

Officer Frank Lam: Head of homicide and forensic analysis

Abby Dollinsy: Victim

Derrick Bell: Boyfriend

Chief Collins: Greensnake Police Chief

The Good and the Bad Cop

Joe Sanie and Samantha Wosilak were patrol partners for more than five years. The two officers have been with the Ohio Greensnake Police Department (OGPD) for seven years. Officer Joe Sanie is from the south, he is strict and he always has his way. There have been a few citizen complaints filed against him since he joined the police department. The complaints were never investigated because the Greensnake Police Chief, Chief Collins, and Officer Joe Sanie have a long standing relationship.

Old Connections

Officer Joe Sanie's father was the patrol partner of Chief Collins while he was alive. Joe Sanie lost his father during a race riot where the police and the minority clashed about a decade ago. Anyone close enough to Officer Joe Sanie would know that he is still bitter by the unfortunate incident. But, with this understanding, Officer Samantha Wosilak often ensures, when possible, that her patrol partner's decisions during officer/suspect encounter are always by the book and consistent with police procedure.

Officer Samantha Wosilak is married to an African American with a six-year-old son named Daniel. Officer Samantha has been described as kind by other officers and citizens. She has received multiple humanitarian awards at the department with State recognition. The patrol work partnership and personality of Officer Joe Sanie and Samantha Wosilak could be best characterized as a good cop/bad cop dynamic.

One Bad Night

Officers Joe Sanie and Samantha Wosilak were on a late night patrol shift. They received a dispatch call to check out what was referred to as a domestic violence incident at the residence of Abby

Dollinsy at 641 Parkview, Lake Shore Drive, Greensnake. Upon arrival, they noticed the door was locked. They knocked and announced their presence to the residents in the house. After repeated knocks with no response, Officer Sanie forced the door open.

The officers cautiously moved into the residence. They observed the living room was in disarray and the house was unnaturally quiet. On high alert, the officers slowly made their way into the kitchen. There, on the floor, lay the motionless body of Abby Dollinsy, in a pool of blood. They called it in for the homicide and forensic analysis division.

The head of homicide and forensic analysis division at the Greensnake P.D. is Officer Frank Lam, who happens to be a good friend of Officer Sanie. The evidence from the scene was gathered and taken to the police department. Abby was a modeling celebrity who worked for a popular local modeling company. The incident caught the attention of the media. Publicity from the case made the Greensnake police department act fast with investigating the homicide.

The Perfect Criminal

The dating life of Abby was not hidden from the public view. Most especially when a beautiful, popular modeling celebrity was in an interracial relationship. The romantic relationship between Abby and Derrick Bell had lasted a year. Derrick is an African American bouncer working at one of the elite night clubs in Greensnake. Derrick has a violent past and a not-so-pleasant record with women, though he has never been convicted.

When drunk, he would make innuendos to the fact that he is a perfect criminal with no trace. Most of the charges against him have been dropped on technicalities or due to lack of evidence. The police interrogated Derrick as the first suspect in the murder of Abby because Derrick was the last person seen with the deceased (at the club) on the night of her murder.

The interrogation led Officer Sanie and Officer Lam, the homicide and forensic analyst, to believe Derrick Bell committed the crime. Unfortunately, they could not find anything at the scene connecting him to the murder. The racial tension, public pressure and the call for justice instigated by the media, increased public focus on the Greensnake P.D.

Planting Evidence

This pressure led Officers Sanie and Lam (homicide) to devise a dishonest means to obtain the DNA of Derrick. They planted his DNA on some of the evidence obtained at the crime scene. This evidence was later used to convict Derrick in the murder of Abby. The DNA helped in discovering another piece of evidence overlooked during the initial investigation, which directly connected Derrick to the murder.

There was racial division on the validity of the verdict. A few minorities connected to the case questioned the validity of the verdict on the notion that the criminal justice system is biased toward men of color. They believed the system often seeks conviction of a black male at all costs, by all means possible.

The department became famous for resolving the murder of Abby. They received grants, awards and recognition from both State and Federal Governments. This included a presidential award for solving a controversial racial case that could have divided the country. All the officers involved in the case were promoted.

A few months later, there was a party at the residence of officer Lam (homicide), where officer Wosilak was present. Officers Wosilak and Sanie, due to the promotions, had not been able to catch up, but they did at the party after a long time. The night was going great with drinking and music. After a few drinks and general catch up, officer Sanie told officer Wosilak about the planting of DNA evidence in the Abby case. He also showed her hard evidence about the planting of the DNA.

Officer Wosilak was shocked. She had her suspicions about the evidence during the investigation, but she could not go further due to the sensitivity, pressure, and popularity of the case. Officer Sanie confirmed her suspicion that night at the party. Officer Sanie also stated that though the

DNA was planted, it helped in locating other evidence that was initially overlooked.

Conviction and Confusion

Officer Wosilak, as a good cop, is torn and does not know what to do, considering that a lot is at stake for the department, the state, and the federal awards, the promotions, the presidential recognition, her family, the officers involved who happen to be white, the previous racial tension, the media involvement, and the community at large.

Though Officer Wosilak is convinced that Derrick is the murderer, but considering her good moral standing and recognition within the department and the community, she is conflicted as to what doing the right thing entails. She is confused about, "what is right?"

The Ethical Dilemma

The ethical dilemma presented in the above scenario requires a careful consideration of relevant facts before any course of action can be suggested and taken. Any course of action taken would have possible consequences. Before diving into the suggestion of possible courses of action that can be taken, it is instructive to examine relevant facts, relevant issues and most importantly, the major issue for determination.

Relevant Ethical Facts

In an attempt to secure the conviction of Derrick in the murder of Abby, Officers Sanie and Lam, the head of homicide and forensic division, devised a dishonest means to obtain and did obtain the DNA of Derrick. They planted the DNA evidence which brought about the conviction of Derrick and also exposed additional evidence which was initially overlooked but directly connected Derrick to the murder. The successful resolution of the case brought about promotions, awards, and recognitions to the Greensnake Police Department.

But, a few months after the conviction of Derrick, there was a party hosted at the residence of Officer Lam (forensic analyst). After few drinks and deep conversation, Officer Sanie told Officer Wosilak about the planted evidence in the case of Derrick. Considering the moral standing of Officer Wosilak, though she is convinced that Derrick committed the murder, she is conflicted as to keeping the secret or reporting the misconduct of Officers Sanie and Lam.

Relevant Ethical Issues

- The uninvestigated complaints against Officer Joe Sanie due to his long standing relationship with his boss, the Greensnake Police Chief.

- The Greensnake Police Department's rapid response to resolving the murder case was not due to the department's reputation but due to the media attention and the publicity of the case.

- Officers Joe Sanie and Frank Lam's dishonest means of obtaining the DNA of Derrick Bell and the planting of evidence. They devised a means to obtain and did obtain the evidence, planted the evidence, seek to secure conviction with the evidence and did secure a conviction.

- The racial divide in the society and also among the supporters of Derrick Bell on the basis of race and the injustice of the criminal justice system.

- The relationship between Officer Samantha Wosilak and Officer Joe Sanie, if such relationship trumps the duty to report the misconduct.

- The silence of Officer Samantha Wosilak on her suspicion about the evidence during investigation.

Without prejudice to all the above relevant ethical issues and points worthy of consideration, the major issue for determination is on what course of action officer Samantha Wosilak should take. Considering what is at stake, and also, the moral standing of officer Samantha Wosilak. The major issue for determination in this scenario is whether officer Samantha Wosilak should report the planting of evidence or not.

Two Options

In this dilemma, there are two major courses of action that are available to officer Wosilak namely: to report, or not to report. It is important to note that there are possible consequences from whatever choice is made. If officer Wosilak decides to report, it is important to examine what the consequences would be.

First, it will pose a question as to if she had any reasonable suspicion at the time, the reasons for her silence at the time was due to the sensitivity, pressure, and popularity of the case. There may be a backlash to her because one could argue that based on her moral standing and recognition, the reasons she gave for a silence at the time are not sufficient or valid enough considering the nature of the case, a murder trial. That is, the life and liberty of Derrick was at stake. Prevention of a possible wrongful conviction of innocence at that time should trump those reasons for someone in her moral standing.

Furthermore, if she decides to report, a lot is at stake for the department because the police department was already famous. They received various grants, awards and recognition from both the states and federal government, including presidential award for resolving a controversial racial case that could have divided the country and cause chaos. Thus, the police department will be under heavy criticism and the status of the grants and awards maybe rescinded. Also, this could cause public unrest, endanger the lives of all personnel working at the Greensnake Police Department.

There will be greater media publicity and also this will deepen racial tension in the country, mistrust in the law enforcement and criminal justice system in general. It will reduce police legitimacy and also strain police-community relationship. Furthermore, it will jeopardize the lives of the family members of the Greensnake Police Department. This could affect the promotions that were connected to this case. There will be a great backlash which the department may not be able to survive. Also, it will affect the relationship between officers Sanie and Wosilak.

There could also be a criminal charge against officers Sanie and Lam. If indicted their police careers are over and they would possibly go to prison. They would be charged with a felony on various counts which include but not limited to conspiracy to obtain evidence illegally, obtaining of evidence illegally, planting of evidence, perjury, conspiracy to secure conviction on illegally obtained evidence, and securing conviction on illegally obtained evidence. These charges could carry more prison time.

There would be a costly investigation into previous cases already closed by department which is not good for the department. This could cost a lot of money. Another consequence, though positive, is that, officer Wosilak through her whistle blowing would be called "hero" and appreciated by the minority community but most likely hated in the police force and by some majority.

The second option is for officer Wosilak not to report the misconduct. This alternative course of action is not exempted from possible consequences either. One of the major consequences is that officer Wosilak would have to constantly struggle with her conscience, considering the kind of person she is, with respect to her moral standing. This could affect overall performance in her work.

There is also a possibility for the "slippery slope effect". This happens when a person makes a bad choice, making it easier to make another bad choice in the future. This is grave because it has been conversed that it is better to let 10 criminals go free than to convict an innocent person. Also, not exposing this misconduct would establish the culture of planting of evidence among those who knew it happened. Thus, an officer will resort to planting of evidence upon a hunch that a suspect is the real perpetrator of the crime when no evidence to establish the connection exists. However, in most cases these hunches maybe false or biased.

Analyzing the Options

Having considered the consequences of the two possible choices, of actions available to officer Wosilak, it is important to state that in view of these circumstances and the arguments for and against respectively, the need for a deeper analysis cannot be overemphasized. Thus, I will proceed to analyze these two available courses of action. I will examine and analyze these courses of action on, justice as due process in the realm of deontology and justice as criminal truth in the realm of teleology. Justice as due process would demand officer Wosilak to speak out and report the misconducts while justice as criminal truth would have her stay silent. I would now examine these theories of moral obligation.

Justice as criminal truth, which would have officer Wosilak remain silent, is a teleological theory. "Teleological theories are consequentialist theories. That is, they are theories which hold that the moral value (including disvalue) of an action or practice is a function of the consequences (real or probable) of that action or practice" (Callahan, 1988, p.19).

This theory is best explained with the utilitarian theory which suggests that the basis of an action should be on the greatest good for the greatest number (Callahan, 1988). Thus, considering the consequences discussed above with respect to officer Wosilak reporting, one could argue that the greatest good for the greatest number of people would demand that she should stay silent.

Reporting would negatively impact more people, actual, real, and known number as opposed to the major arguments for reporting the misconduct is predicated, which is preventing unknown, probable future innocent conviction. Reporting would impact the police departments in its entirety, including their relatives. The likelihood of civil unrest is high and thus, it will deepen racial tension and it will affect the trust and legitimacy of the law enforcement and the criminal justice system in general.

The possible implication or consequences of reporting is real, known and very predictable. Thus, from a teleological standpoint, reporting the misconduct would not be in the interest of the greatest good for the greatest number. Furthermore, another teleological stance is the theory of ethical egoism. By ethical egoism, "it is the view that the agent should choose that (act, rule) which will (tend to) produce the greatest good for the agent choosing" (Callahan, 1988, p. 19).

In this instance, what does officer Wosilak have at stake, as the acting agent. Officer

Wosilak would lose many friends, most importantly her former patrol partner, officer Sanie. Sending a dear friend to prison and ruining their career may be such a big burden that officer Wosilak may not be prepared for. Also there will be a backlash which may affect officer Wosilak's family. Such backlash includes and not limited to death threats, physical and emotional attacks, media pressure, attention and undue popularity.

These consequences would directly affect negatively the life of officer Wosilak. This is not an attempt to argue that reporting does not have any good but the arguments here are that such acts cannot produce a greater good or the greatest good for the acting agent. In view of the above, ethical egoism would also demand that officer Wosilak should be silent and not report the misconduct as the acting agent.

On the second available option to officer Wosilak, which is to report, the deontological stance would agree with this choice. That is, justice as due process. "The deontologist denies that the moral value of actions or practices is exclusively a function of the (real or probable) consequences of those actions or practices" (Callahan, 1988, p. 19-20). That is, consequences do not have any relevance in moral evaluation of actions or practices. Thus, when rules are made, consequences do not matter at that point anymore. "Once moral rule is established, it is exceptionless" (Callahan, 1988, p. 20).

Justice as due process would demand that the trial and conviction of Derrick should follow due process of the law, of which planting of evidence, securing DNA through unconventional ways failed to meet the due process requirements. Therefore, Officer Wosilak has a duty to report. In this instance, strict deontological stance provides no other choice than to report. Furthermore, reporting would prevent the occurrence of similar incidences in the near future; also preventing the conviction of an innocent person on the bases of comparable police misconduct. Furthermore, the moderate deontological view holds that as agents:

"We have a number of prima facie duties, or duties which can come into conflict with one another, in any given concrete situation, two or more of these duties might come into conflict and the task in being moral is to discern which of our conflicting duties takes priority in that concrete situation" (Callahan, 1988, p. 20).

Thus, based on the moderates view, one could argue that Officer Wosilak has a duty to her patrol partner and also a duty to possible innocent person who may be wrongly convicted in the future on the bases of this kind of police misconduct.

One could further argue that the duty to any future possible innocent person to be convicted is superior to the duty officer Wosilak owes her patrol partner. Weighing these duties and moral responsibilities, it is compelling for officer Wosilak to report this police misconduct of her patrol partner. Also officer Wosilak's conscience, personal peace, and unrest from not reporting could produce a more compelling reason for her to report considering her ethical record and standing.

Choosing a Course of Action

It is difficult to choose between the two causes of action available to officer Wosilak as both present a challenging dilemma. However, having examined the available options in line with theories of moral obligation, I am more persuaded by the argument and position as set forth by the teleological stance advising officer Wosilak to remain silent and not report the police misconduct of her patrol partner in the trial and conviction of Derrick.

They predicated their arguments on the greatest good for the greatest number (Callahan, 1988). They relied on this notion and argue that considering the consequences of reporting which they referred to as grave; reporting would not serve the greatest good to the greatest number. The teleological stance in the advice of officer Wosilak further coveys that reporting would negatively impact more people, actual, real and known as opposed to probable or future innocent person's conviction.

They further stated that reporting would negatively impact the Greensnake Police Department, department's image, reputation, and also all personnel working in the department. They would be at risk and danger of physical injury, including their relatives. They further argue that such action would undermine the police-citizen trust, and legitimacy. Also, it would deepen the racial tension thereby creating civil unrest in the larger society.

I am persuaded by this argument. It is important to note that the greatest good must serve the greatest number. In this instance, it is a known fact that the race relation of police and citizen is not cordial and the teleologists may not be wrong to asset that by reporting, this would deepen existing racial problem, thereby creating civil unrest. To me, this is a concern serious enough to consider. Considering all that would be affected by reporting, the advice or the choice preferred from the teleological stance is reasonable and I am persuaded by the logic of this reasoning.

Furthermore, the teleologists argued on ethical egoism, that officer Wosilak should choose that act that would produce the greatest good for her as the acting agent. They argued that reporting would not produce the greatest good for officer

Wosilak, while believing that she would be affected negatively. However, they pointed out that there might be a good thing in reporting but such good does not amount to greatest good after careful consideration.

I agree with this argument. Officer Wosilak would receive a lot of media attention capable of putting her private life in danger. This danger could extend to her family as a result of negative media popularity. I find myself agreeing with the demand of ethical egoism, advising Officer Wosilak to fail to report and stay silent.

However, deontological stance suggests that officer Wosilak should report on the basis of due process. Their notion is predicated on preventing an innocent from falling victim of this police misconduct. They relied on the notion that it is better to allow ten criminals to go free than to punish one innocent person. They further argue that silence and not reporting would make this possible. Also, it would create a police culture of planting of evidence and obtaining conviction in unjust ways.

This argument seems very appealing, but I am not persuaded because in this case, Derrick is not an innocent man. This argument would have been a little more compelling if Derrick were actually innocent. The stakes are high here and consequences of reporting would outweigh not reporting. If Derrick was innocent, the conclusion arrived here might change. I may arrive at a different conclusion.

Furthermore, the teleologists contend that the consequence of reporting in this case is real, predictable, actual, and known as opposed to the argument of the deontologist which suggests following the rule without exception and in this case there by making the protection of possible future innocent person possible. Without disregarding protection of the possible innocent person, I agree with the arguments made in support of not reporting that there is difference between knowing the direct, real, and known consequences of an action compared to predicting a probable future person. One consequence is more certain and immediate than the other. Thus, consequences of reporting is more certain, immediate, real and known than the possible effects of not reporting.

Also, it is important to note that "contemporary deontologists tend to allow that consequences (particularly bad consequences which can be avoided) are morally important" (Callahan, 1988, p. 20). It is without a doubt that this scenario established the fact that reporting would create more immediate and imminent negative consequences than not reporting. To that I find the teleological argument more appealing and I am greatly persuaded thereby. In view of the above, I will hold that officer Wosilak should stay silent and not report as justice as criminal truth would have her stay silent.

Other Relevant Ethical Issues Identified

Having examined and determined the main issue for determination, it is noteworthy to briefly consider other relevant ethical issues and points identified in this ethical dilemma. One ethical issue is with the uninvestigated complaints against officer Sanie due to his long-standing relationship with his boss, the Greensnake Police Chief.

This could be explained under the ethic of care which focuses on the demands of relationship. The chief is most likely aware that investigating such a complaint may not be good for officer Sanie. It is a sense of loyalty. "An ethics of caring require fidelity to persons, a willingness to acknowledge their right to be who they are, an openness to encountering them in their authentic individuality, a loyalty to the relationship" (Starratt, 1991, p. 195). The ethics of care could also be inferred from the relationship that exists between Officers Sanie and Wosilak.

The deep personal conversation, the vulnerability and the information on planting of evidence could be argued to stem from a more loyal and trusting relationship that both Officers had established over time. Furthermore, officer Wosilak has often ensured when possible that her partner's decision during officer/suspect encounter is consistent with police procedure. Also, the silence of officer Wosilak on her suspicions about the inconsistencies in the evidence during investigation and trial could be explained under the ethics of care and ethics of critique.

Her relationship with the police force and the department trump her suspicions. She could not put herself in a place to criticize the department or destroy her loyalty to the department. Although, it is interesting to envisage that ethic of care would be used to defend silence, essentially a cover-up.

Also one can note the ethic of critique in the Greensnake Police Department's rapid response to resolving the murder case which was not due to the department's attribute, but due to the media attention and the publicity of the case. The racial divide in the society and between the supporters of Derrick on the basis of race and the skepticism about the criminal justice could be argued under the ethic of critique and justice.

There is need to address injustice in the society and the call for equality in treatment of members of the society by the criminal justice system, irrespective of race. Thus, with respect to ethic of justice, the minority and the supporters of Derrick are trying to protect and preserve their self-interests against wrongful convictions and the bias of the criminal justice system in general. Furthermore, officers Sanie and Lam's dishonest means of obtaining the DNA of Derrick and the planting of evidence contravene justice as a due process.

Justice, as a due process, demands that proper process should be taken. The law is expected to be followed irrespective of how or what the officer feels, thinks, or wants. It is important to note that though the DNA was planted, other evidence connected Derrick to the murder. Although, it could be argued that the end justified the means since Derrick was not an innocent man. Justice as criminal truth will show some deference to the officers while justice as due process would not.

Final Thoughts

As seen in the analysis of this ethical dilemma, deciding between which courses of action to choose is not an easy task. There are possible consequences with any course of action one decides to take. Thus, a critical evaluation cannot be overemphasized.

Deciding to report comes along with various consequences that could have a lasting effect, in this instance a negative effect.

On the other hand, deciding to stay silent also comes with its consequences, which on the long run could jeopardize the law, order, and due process and thereby creating a police culture that would be threatening to all. Notwithstanding the difficulty in deciding which course of action to take, with a careful thought, and on the strength of arguments, one could come to a logical conclusion on which course of action is preferable in a given circumstance after considering the facts in whole.

This scenario has presented a difficult ethical dilemma and the analysis has presented a preferable course of action. Thus, considering the arguments for and against the available courses of action, Officer Samantha Wosilak is advised to stay silent based on the aforementioned relevant ethical considerations.

References

Callahan, J.C. (Ed.). (1988). Ethical issues in professional life. New York: Oxford University Press.

Starratt R.J. (1991). Building an ethical school: A theory for practice in educational leadership. Educational Administration Quarterly, 27, 185-202

Ethical Dilemmas

Chapter 6

The Caseworker's Dilemma

By Lakishia Huggins
Toledo, Ohio

Definitions:

Job & Family Services: provides services such as temporary cash assistance, food stamps, and Medicaid, subsidized child care, adult protection, disability assistance and prevention, retention and contingency services

Caseworker: is a type of social worker who is employed by a government agency, non-profit organization, or another group to take on the cases of individuals and provide them with advocacy, information or other services

Medical Assistance: Medicaid (medical assistance) provides health care coverage to families who may not otherwise have access to health care. The program is designed to safeguard the health and well-being of residents, particularly children, pregnant women, elderly, and individuals with disabilities.

Processing Applications: refers to reviewing applications to determine eligibility for benefits

Characters:

Kelly: main character

Joan: minor character

The Caseworker's Dilemma

Kelly and Joan were like sisters. They had been neighbors and friends for more than 10 years. Joan was affectionately known as Ms. Joan by Kelly's daughters, whom she watched mature into beautiful young ladies. She adored the girls, and Joan as if she had known them her whole life. In many ways Kelly and Joan felt more like family than friends.

Employment and Unemployment

Joan was an executive director for a local nonprofit organization that was heavily involved in their community. Although she often felt overworked, she truly enjoyed her job. Kelly, on the other hand, recently lost her job due to downsizing and had been feverishly looking for a new position. However, she kept herself occupied by volunteering on the board of directors for the agency where Joan worked. It was a perfect fit.

As Kelly became more involved with the board, she began to realize the organization was in severe financial trouble. It was so critical that several major decisions had to be made. As fate would have it, Joan would be laid off per the board of directors a couple months before the Thanksgiving holiday. While it was hard, Joan accepted their decision and gladly welcomed the idea of having some time off. She decided collecting unemployment couldn't be that bad.

As Joan began collecting unemployment, Kelly's unemployment benefits were unfortunately coming to an end. She had looked everywhere for full or even part-time employment opportunities.

Good News

Finally, after months of submitting resumes, it happened. Kelly was offered a temporary position with Job & Family Services as a caseworker where she would determine eligibility for those clients applying for medical assistance. She was happy and looked forward to being a working woman again.

After a few months of getting acclimated to the job Kelly became very familiar with the internal workings of the agency. She was well liked by her coordinator as well as the other caseworkers in her unit. Her processing skill set was proficient, which made the position even better. Little to her surprise, she was offered a permanent position.

That evening Kelly called Joan to share the good news. But, when she answered Kelly knew something was wrong. Kelly had known Joan so well that she could tell in the sound of her voice if there was an issue. Joan quickly asked if Kelly could come over to her house to talk. Whatever it was, Kelly knew it could not be good.

Very Bad News

On the drive to Joan's house Kelly was a nervous wreck. Her stomach was in knots and her palms were sweaty. In the last month Joan had endured unimaginable tragedy. She had lost her mother to cancer and shortly after lost her uncle. Kelly was praying there was not another death in the family. As she pulled into the driveway she could see the door was already open, and Joan was standing there. Kelly paused a bit as she turned off her car and slowly exited the vehicle.

She could see that Joan had been crying. "I don't know if I can take anymore Kelly" said Joan. Kelly reached out to hug her. They held hands as they walked inside and sat on the couch. Joan took a deep breath began to speak. "The doctor called today to tell me the lumps in my breast have them concerned. They want to remove them in two weeks."

Kelly sat quietly. She knew that Joan was scared given her family's history with cancer. But she was also upset because her insurance coverage would be ending on Friday. Neither of them said a word, they just sat and watched the fish swim in the fish tank.

A week later, Joan decided that she had to do all that she could to get some type of insurance before her procedure. She didn't know where to begin. She never had to worry about this kind of thing because she always had a job. She always had benefits. She had been in pretty good health. Then it hit her. She would have to apply for medical assistance with Job & Family Services. If she could at least get the application completed and filled out they might possibly back date the start of service to the date of application. It was worth a try she thought.

The Meeting

When Kelly got to work on Tuesday her coordinator announced that there would be a meeting in the afternoon to go over some policies for the unit. It wasn't often they had meetings on a Tuesday, so it must be important. After lunch, Kelly headed to the conference room to take a seat before they got started with the meeting. When she got there Linda, a coworker, was headed to take a seat as well. "Hi Kelly!" said Linda. Kelly spoke as she made her way to the first row. She asked if Linda knew what the meeting was about. Linda explained a caseworker was accused of processing applications out of sequence. He managed to make sure that applications of people he knew were completed in one day even if they had just been submitted. The agency's rule was that if you came across an application for someone you knew, that you should give it to the coordinator. Kelly thought that wouldn't be an issue for her. She didn't know anyone that needed medical assistance.

The meeting lasted for about an hour and then all caseworkers were instructed to go back to work. When Kelly got to her desk she could see that the mail clerk had delivered more applications. As she started to put them in order alphabetically, she noticed a name that was familiar. She blinked twice and then again. The application was for Joan. Joan Miller. Her friend, her neighbor, her sister.

Dilemma Analysis

Kelly is faced with a challenging ethical dilemma. Should she push through the application of a dear friend facing cancer treatment? In some ways this could be considered a life and death decision. Or, should she follow the rules and hope for the best for her friend Joan? Two solutions will be discussed through the ethic of justice and the ethic of care.

Solution #1 - Ethic of Justice

Considering that Kelly is a board member/public service employee she understands the importance of policies and procedures. Her first thought was to be concerned about following the rules. She recognizes that the policy around processing applications is in place to avoid situations of favoritism and to allow for equal access to medical benefits.

But, her friend is faced with a life-threatening disease. And so, the ethic of justice comes into play. Should she process the application as if she doesn't know Joan or follow protocol? According to Starratt (1991) an ethic of justice provides more of a candid response, even though the response may itself be flawed.

In this solution, Kelly would acknowledge that the application is one of an individual that she is acquainted with and make her coordinator aware of this situation. Some would say that she did the right thing, followed the agency's policy, and did not jeopardize her job.

However, with this approach it works out well for Kelly but what about Joan? Even in the pursuit to do what's fair someone will suffer to some degree. This then creates a circumstance where there is conflict between conventional and reflective morality.

Conventional morality is to be guided by the traditional or customary rules without criticizing the rule itself. On the other hand, reflective morality occurs when an individual begins to think about his or her actions, especially when those actions involve the interests of other persons (Callahan, 1988). Kelly internally will be confronted by the fact of blindly obeying the orders and Joan obtaining medical coverage in enough time to save her life. She believes that this will be the least problematic and morally compromising resolution.

However, according to Howe, Kelly will be just fine. From his perspective she is taking on an Liberal Egalitarian standpoint, that is the principle of equal opportunity. Rawls (as cited by Howe, 1971) states that equal opportunity is required for individuals to have a fair chance to enjoy a reasonable amount of society's goods. This theory believes that it is not the fault of the individual that they need help. Therefore, social agencies are required to have practices in place to allow for this to occur. So, by not altering the procedure of processing applications she is allowing for everyone to have equal access to medical assistance, which is a good thing.

Solution #2 - Ethic of Care

Relationships are important to Kelly, especially the one she has with Joan. Her first thought was to quickly process the application, get it entered in the system, and move on to the next one as if nothing was ever wrong. She feels as if the next steps are crucial for Joan's road to recovery and hesitation is unacceptable. And so, the ethic of caring comes into play. According to Starratt (1991) an ethic of caring provides faithfulness. It implies a level of concern that honors the dignity of each person and desires to see that person enjoy a fully human life.

In this solution, Kelly would not acknowledge that the application is one of an individual that she is acquainted with and process it. Some would say that she did the right thing; that she did a small deed to save a life and no one was hurt.

However, with this approach it works out well for Joan but what about the individuals who had submitted applications before Joan? Even in the process to save her friend others are in need of medical insurance. This then creates a circumstance where there is conflict in how she arrived at this moral judgement.

According to Callahan (1988) moral argument may involve inconsistencies in taking opinions on various ethical questions issues. In one instance, Kelly holds that the process is fair and understands the policy related to determining eligibility for applicants, but also wants to allow for reviewing the applications of those who are facing life-threatening illnesses first. Kelly, within herself, has good reasons for making the choice that she did. In her mind, she is helping not only Joan but her children as well. She believes that this will be the most problematic and morally compromising resolution.

Conversely, Howe would argue that Kelly's actions were justified fully. It his eyes she would undoubtedly be a libertarian. Libertarians (Nozick, 1974, as cited by Howe) deem liberty as the overriding value, and maximizing it is the best way to avoid showing disrespect for persons' dignity by treating them paternalistically. Although Joan had taken the necessary steps in applying for assistance Kelly felt as if it would be in her best interest to ensure that Joan's application was approved. If she had not, who knows how long it would have taken to be accepted, and time was not an opponent that Joan could afford to battle.

Strike would also agree with Howe. He would offer explanation for Kelly by way of The Principle of Benefit Maximization. According to Strike (2005) whenever we are faced with a choice, the best and most just decision is the one that results in the most good or the greatest benefit for the person. He would even offer that The Principal of Equal Respect would come into play. This prospective says that we would treat others as the way we would have them treat us. Given the relationship that Kelly and Joan have, it is a given that Kelly feels if the shoe were on the other foot, Joan would do the same for her.

References

Callahan, J. C. (1988). Basics and background. In J. C. Callahan (ed.), *Ethical Issues in Professional Life*. New York: Oxford University Press.

Howe, K. R. (1993). The liberal democratic tradition and educational ethics. In Strike & Ternasky (eds.), *Ethics for Professionals in Education* (Chapter 2, pp. 27-42).

Starratt, R. J. (1991). Building an ethical school: A theory for practice in educational leadership. *Educational Administration Quarterly*, 27(2), 185-202.

Strike, K. A., Haller, E. J., & Soltis, J. F. (2005). *The ethics of school administration* (3rd ed.). New York: Teachers College Pres

Ethical Dilemmas

Chapter 7

Friends in High Places

by Andy Alt
Bowling Green, Ohio

Definitions:
Student Government Association: Student-led group responsible to advocate for student interests and concerns

First Generation: Signifies a student is first in their family to attend college

Public University: College receiving government funds with the primary purpose of serving the educational needs of the students within the state

Characters:
Allen Soltis: President of Trilling State University (TSU)

Delores Crawford: Vice President of Student Success and Enrollment

Dr. Bethany Haverdink: Assistant Vice President for Student Success

Thad Sidebothom: SGA President

Mr. Henry Tilton: Thad's Internship Coordinator

Friends in High Places

Trilling State University (TSU) is mid-sized public university in the mid-West. Highly dependent on state funding and enrollment, increased pressure for retaining students has led to the development of several initiatives and programs designed to support student success. Approximately 1/3 of undergraduate students are first-generation, and 20% are fully Pell Eligible.

In light of retention data suggesting that a number of students are unable to continue at TSU due to financial concerns, University President Allen Soltis and the Foundation Board have designated funding to assist students with financial difficulty. These "Retention and Completion Grants" are earmarked for students with strong academic performance (over 3.0 GPA) financial need as demonstrated by students' FAFSA (EFC under $12,000), and in good academic and conduct standing.

While the University leadership and Student Government Association (SGA) have typically enjoyed a positive relationship, recent incidents related to student organization funding policies, questions about leadership support for diversity and inclusion efforts, and growing concerns of student safety have created relational struggles and conflict between SGA and University administration. The SGA has been suspected by University leadership of promulgating opposition among the student body and even some key faculty serving in shared governance positions.

Character Introduction

One of the most tenured members of cabinet at TSU, Ms. Delores Crawford serves as the Vice President for Student Success and Enrollment (VPSSE). In this role, Ms. Crawford is responsible for admissions, retention, and graduation efforts for undergraduate students. With a multi-year decline in key metrics in those areas and a subsequent decline in state funding, President Soltis has expressed very firm expectations for the VPSSE.

In an attempt to improve student success, the VPSSE changed scholarship renewal policies (including increased requirements for maintaining university scholarships: GPA and credit hours). This has unexpectedly received criticism from students for changing, further complicating the relationship between the VPSEE and the President.

The VPSSE, also looking for some "wins" with the President and SGA, is eager to create guidelines and implement disbursement policies related to the newly created the Completion Grants. The VPSSE has charged Assistant Vice President for Student Success Dr. Bethany Haverdink with operationalizing this effort. Dr. Haverdink is relatively new to TSU but fully aware of the tension between the President and her VP. In her role, she chairs the Scholarship Review Committee, receives scholarship appeals and other "special" financial considerations, and under the guidelines she established for the "Completion Grants" determines eligibility, identifies and selects recipients, and awards funds for the completion grant.

The current SGA President is Thad Sidebothom, a highly active student, well-known among students, University administrators, and University Trustees. As a first-generation student with little family support, Thad is fully reliant on scholarship funding. In fact, Thad's mother is a single-parent, ill and unable to work.

As SGA President he receives a substantial stipend for serving in this leadership position. In addition to this stipend, Thad is receiving another merit scholarship for his high school academic performance. A social work major, Thad recently completed a semester in which he was working to satisfy an internship requirement. Thad is a continuing Senior with a cumulative GPA of 2.8, on track to graduate in 2 semesters (Spring and Summer), following his internship. He is eager to graduate, and soon, as he has a guaranteed post-graduation job-offer. The offer comes from a vocal

University Trustee and he is scheduled to begin employment in August, immediately after summer graduation.

Due to his mother's illness, Thad has been sending his excess scholarship money home to support mom and sister. Given his GPA, the new scholarship guidelines are likely to impact him greatly at the end of this semester.

Thad's Internship Coordinator is Mr. Henry Tilton. Mr. Tilton is in his second semester at TSU and unware of less familiar grading policies, and certainly unfamiliar with newly introduced scholarship requirements. As Internship Coordinator, Mr. Tilton is responsible for verifying internship hours for each student enrolled this term, as well as assigning a final grade and assessment for each student at the end of the term.

Lost Time

Due to his busy schedule and incredibly demanding expectations as SGA President, Thad Sidebothom struggled through his internship and was challenged in completing required hours. As a result, he occasionally overslept and arrived late, and sometimes also left early. Although he began missing scheduled internship hours, Thad continued to report them as completed on his internship log.

His on-site internship supervisor was initially unaware, but began to notice Thad's pattern of arriving late or leaving early and confronted him. Thad's response was honest, yet while he garnered the supervisor's sympathy, the supervisor did notify the TSU Internship Coordinator. Mr. Tilton.

Aware of Thad's connections and profile among the leadership and Trustees, Mr. Tilton chose to not report the alleged academic misconduct out of empathy and fear of retaliation. Instead, and after speaking with Thad, Mr. Tilton recorded an Incomplete grade.

Although Thad's grade was not immediately affected, he did not fulfill requirements to change the incomplete grade in a timely manner. Eventually, his grade turned into an F. This grade change then resulted in Thad's cumulative GPA dropping to 2.45, which impacted his scholarship under the new requirements, put his role as SGA

President at risk (required GPA is 2.75), and caused a near certain delay in graduation by another semester, jeopardizing employability with Trustee.

Political Leverage

Recognizing his connection and leverage among university administration and leadership, Thad contacted the President's Office and requested that his scholarship be reinstated fully, and the internship requirement be waived because he had completed "most" of the required hours.

The TSU President referred the matter to the VPSSE. Viewing this as an opportunity to repair some of the relationship between herself and the SGA and also win some points with the University President, the VPSSE passed this on to the AVP and implied that she should strongly consider reinstating the scholarship and "work something out" regarding the internship requirement to help Thad graduate on-time.

Dilemma and Ethical Considerations

Following the conversation with her VP, Dr. Haverdink began to do some additional fact-finding and spoke with the student and Internship

Coordinator, Mr. Tilton. In her discussion with Thad, she learned of his family's financial and health challenges and also Thad's upcoming employment opportunity. In speaking with Thad and Mr. Tilton, it was not until this time that she became aware of the apparent unreported case of academic misconduct for Thad's falsification of his internship log. According to university policy, the reporting of the misconduct must come from the instructor of record, in this case, Mr. Tilton.

Faced with what she understood to be a quite complicated matter, she carefully considered the various options and solutions in front her, and scribbled the following questions and thoughts on her office white-board:

- Do I have a duty to persuade the instructor to report the misconduct?
- Are there other grading policies that might allow for an Incomplete grade to be issued, and could Thad complete the remaining hours?
- What about the value and integrity of a TSU degree?

- Do I have a responsibility to Thad's family? Without this scholarship, will they have enough financial means to pay rent or medical bills?

- Thad's had a hard life and has overcome many obstacles to get to this point.

- Is waiving a requirement fair to other students who have completed their internship hours?

- I cannot avoid bringing this to the scholarship review committee; what might I say to them?

- How would I even begin to waive an internship requirement?

- What damage could any of these decisions do to the relationships between students and administrators, among students themselves, administration and the Trustees, myself and my colleagues at TSU and beyond?

- To what extent is my job on the line? Which decisions compromise my employment? My integrity?

- What about my personal code of ethics?

- Is there a right way through this? No way seems clean or easy.

As a former student conduct administrator, Dr. Haverdink thought that an evaluation of the known facts would be useful, and she began to make another list next to these questions on her board:

- Scholarship Policy: 3.0 GPA; appeals process: letter explaining challenges

- Academic Misconduct: reported by instructor

- Internships are graded "Pass/Fail"

- Social Work requirement: 300 on-site hours (Thad appears to have completed 255)

- Degree requirements waived only by Department Chair

- Grade policy: Incomplete course requirements must be satisfied within 2 months of term-end

- Thad's family situation: single mom, sick; young sister; financial challenges

- Thad's employment with Trustee: life-changing trajectory

Dr. Haverdink realizes that there is no way to avoid making a decision, recalls reading in her doctoral program about "ethics being part of the job" and "dilemmas involving sacrifice of something significant", accepts that she may be viewed as unjust, unfair, or inefficient, and sets to work at evaluating her available solutions through some serious reflective equilibrium and past professional experience.

Solution 1

Finding security and familiarity in relying on policy and procedure, her first inclination is to consider a scenario in which Thad is required to submit a scholarship appeal and also navigate the process related to completing his outstanding and incomplete academic requirements. She recognizes that none of these decisions (e.g. filing an academic honesty complaint, reinstating a scholarship, or waiving a degree requirement) are fully under her singular authority, and believes that this may be the least complicated solution, as well as the least morally compromising for herself.

In this solution, she leans heavily on three similar ethical frameworks: the Ethic of Justice, the Principle of Equal Treatment, and a Consequentialist approach of decision making. A justice-based framework relies on the various rules and policies which apply in this situation, and might be uniformly applied to other future cases. The question of "how to govern" is answered by through a review of scholarship and academic program requirements, as well as appropriate and available appeals procedures.

Dr. Haverdink's appreciation for this approach is rooted in the security that such policies allow administrators to make both routine and complex decisions with more consistency and fairness. Under the Principle of Equal Treatment, Thad's family, financial, and future circumstances are quite irrelevant. This principle would suggest that all past students, current students, and future students should be treated the same if they were to fail to meet academic requirements.

Of course, she cannot reason without being mindful of the consequences for everyone involved. From a consequential perspective, Dr. Haverdink considers the various possible outcomes for Thad, herself, and future students. In thinking about whether helping Thad by somewhat unilaterally waiving requirements serves the greater good of the university community, she quickly arrives at the conclusion that it would not. The value of a TSU degree is predicated on those degrees signifying that students have fully met requirements. Taking to somewhat of an extreme, if word got out that TSU did not hold students to their degree requirements, future TSU grads might have difficulty gaining employment upon graduation.

Although her decision to follow policy to the letter may result in Thad possibly losing his scholarship (and Dr. Haverdink possibly losing her job), it is in following the established policies and procedures which helps to ensure that future situations can be handled similarly, and that the integrity of the institution and educational mission remains in-tact. In effect, these policies and procedures serve as safeguards for everyone involved. Utilitarianism, she recalls, precludes providing special privileges to anyone, regardless of whether they are the SGA President, well-connected to the Trustees, or in a unique and difficult financial situation.

Solution 2

In the spirit of due process and giving all parties an opportunity to present their version of events, Dr. Haverdink then considers a solution in which she exerts her full authority to resolve Thad's situation with singular attention to the various and specific circumstances of his case. Not insensitive to Thad's family situation, she mentally exercises some Situational Appreciation, considers applying an Ethic of Care, and gives less weight to the consequentialist perspective. In this scenario she would reinstate his scholarship as well as arrange for a way to also waive the incomplete academic requirement.

Although leaning on policy and procedure is safe and allows for a more methodical resolution, she is convinced that the facts of this case are not necessarily cut and dry. In fact, by knowing more about the circumstances (including his family situation and the implications on his professional future), she begins to realize that she might be able to make a more informed and justifiable decision. These, facts she believes, might be the most salient features of the situation. With these features and facts clearly delineated in her mind, she believes that she might be best able to judge the situation and make a defensible decision in Thad's favor.

Although she does not have any relationship with Thad prior to this situation, Dr. Haverdink believes strongly in an Ethic of Care. She holds her personal and professional relationships in high regard, and often reflects on the thought of "what her relationships demand of her". Thad, she argues with herself, is a student, one of which she has a general and somewhat theoretical relationship with every undergraduate student.

As a student affairs and higher education practitioner, she believes that she might be obligated to provide a full extent of care to students in a situation such as Thad's, without regard to rules or regulations. Furthermore, recognizing Thad's dignity as a young man attempting to reach his potential while also selflessly serving his family and caring for his mother, she begins to consider that a non-consequentialist resolution of this situation may be best.

Solution 3

After giving further and more considerable thought to her second solution, and upon thinking deeply about her own moral principles and personal code, it occurs to her that there may be a way to demonstrate a full ethic of care, follow the stated policies and procedures in an ethic of justice. Although she is relatively new to TSU, she has quickly developed a trusted network of faculty and administrators, many whom she believes will understand her desire to help this student while also honoring the ethic of justice and practical value of following a set of administrative policies and procedures.

By leveraging her relationships with faculty and administrators and employing her knowledge of policies and procedures, she decides that it is within her purview to connect with the Internship Coordinator to clarify and resolve misconduct procedures, coach Thad through a written scholarship appeal, help him through negotiating and arranging a means for him to complete his remaining 45 internship hours, and still graduate on-time in order for Thad to begin employment with the Trustee at the agreed upon time in August.

Conclusion

In an educational environment where rules, regulations, and policies are perhaps as necessary in governing as are administrators and administrative bodies with moral agency and decision-making authority, complex scenarios where decisions are weighed and made on the Ethics of Justice and Care are unavoidable. Often, these types of scenarios call into question personal codes of ethics and challenge the decision-makers by also challenging their own moral values.

An understanding of and ability to apply principles of maximum benefit and equal respect, as well as consequential/non-consequential reasoning skills are critical to an educational leader. Reflective equilibrium and situational appreciation is also essential. When there is no clear or clean way through a complex situation, these various ethical principles and reflective practices may serve as the only viable road-map for leaders to bring these situations to resolution.

ABOUT THE AUTHOR

 David Thorne is a pastor, writer, speaker, husband, and father of three active boys. He graduated from the University of Mary Washington with a degree in psychology. He has earned master's degrees from Regent University and Western Governor's University. His degrees are in practical theology, human services counseling, and management and leadership. David has completed course work for a leadership studies doctoral degree at Bowling Green State University and is currently working on his dissertation . His research will focus on effective volunteer management and leadership.

Contact: drairwolf@me.com
Website: www.davidthorne.me

Ethical Dilemmas